# Comprehension and Language Arts Skills

## Level 5

A Division of The McGraw-Hill Companies

Columbus, Ohio

**www.sra4kids.com**

*SRA/McGraw-Hill*

*A Division of The McGraw·Hill Companies*

Send all inquiries to:
SRA/McGraw-Hill
8787 Orion Place
Columbus, OH  43240-4027

Printed in the United States of America.

ISBN  0-07-571905-3

**10 11 12 13 14 15 POH 08 07 06 05**

# Table of Contents

# Drawing Conclusions

**Focus**  Good readers know how to **draw conclusions** about characters or events they read about in a story.

> **Drawing conclusions** means putting information together to make a statement about a character or event in a story. Readers can draw conclusions based on
> ▶ how a character behaves or what he or she says.
> ▶ how characters react to each other.
> ▶ when and where a story takes place.
> While a conclusion may not be directly stated in the text, it should be supported by examples in the story.

## Identify

Look through "Class President." What conclusions can you draw about a character or event in the story? In the spaces provided, write your conclusion and the page number on which its supporting information can be found.

**1.** Page: _____

Conclusion about a character: _____

Information that supports the conclusion: _____

_____

**2.** Page: _____

Conclusion about an event: _____

Information that supports the conclusion: _____

_____

**UNIT 1** Cooperation and Competition • **Lesson 1** *Class President*

▶ **Drawing Conclusions**

## Practice and Apply

Think of the names of three things, such as a computer, a horse, and a soccer ball. Then, write three statements about each thing, without using the things' names. (Use the word "it" instead.)

**1.** _____

_____

_____

**2.** _____

_____

_____

**3.** _____

_____

_____

Show your statements to a classmate. See whether your classmate can draw the right conclusions and identify the things you wrote about.

COMPREHENSION

# Nouns

| Rule | Example |
|---|---|
| ▶ A **common noun** names any person, place, thing, or idea. A **proper noun** names a particular person, place, or thing. A proper noun is always capitalized. | ▶ teacher<br>Mr. Alvarez |
| ▶ Most nouns can be made plural by simply adding *-s*. Words that end with *s*, *x*, *z*, *ch*, or *sh* form the plural by adding *-es*. | ▶ cat—cats<br>class—classes |
| ▶ Words that end in a consonant and *y* form the plural by changing the *y* to *i* and adding *-es*. Some words that end in *f* or *fe* are made plural by changing the *f* to *v* and adding *-es*. | ▶ penny—pennies<br>leaf—leaves |
| ▶ A few nouns completely change their form when made plural. | ▶ child—children |

**Circle the nouns in this paragraph.**

The giant sequoias of California started growing centuries ago from seeds the size of a grain of wheat. Some of the trees are up to 300 feet tall and have bark that is four feet thick. The General Sherman is the largest tree in the world. It is in Sequoia National Park, which is near Fresno.

► **Nouns**

GRAMMAR AND USAGE

**Practice**

**Write the plural form of each noun.**

1. shirt _____
2. watch _____
3. fly _____
4. shelf _____
5. goose _____
6. nurse _____
7. day _____
8. sash _____
9. buzz _____
10. gas _____

**Proofread**

**Draw three lines under letters that should be capital letters. Draw a slash through letters that should be small letters.**

We are learning about mexico in school. Did You know that nearly 96 million People live in Mexico? Mexico's official Language is spanish. The capital and largest City in Mexico is mexico City. It is located on the same spot as the ancient aztec capital of Tenochtitlán. The flag of Mexico shows an eagle sitting on a Cactus holding a snake in its beak. The color green in the flag stands for Independence.

# Making Inferences

**Focus** When writers don't include all the information about a character or a story event, readers must **make inferences** in order to get the whole picture.

Readers can use information from a story, along with their own experience or knowledge, to **make inferences** that help them understand a character or event more completely.

## Identify

Find two sentences in "The Marble Champ" that give you some information about Lupe. Write the page numbers and sentences. Then, write a word or phrase that would describe Lupe's character, based on the sentences you wrote.

**1.** Page: _____

Sentence: _____

_____

What the reader can infer about Lupe from this sentence: _____

_____

**2.** Page: _____

Sentence: _____

_____

What the reader can infer about Lupe from this sentence: _____

_____

▶ **Making Inferences**

**Practice**

Read the paragraph below. Then, write down what you can infer about the person in the paragraph.

Most of the time Marty kept his eyes down and looked at his desk. If, by accident, someone did catch his eye, he always blushed furiously and looked away immediately. When the teacher asked a question, Marty would sometimes raise his hand. But when the teacher called on him, no one could understand what he was saying because he spoke so softly.

Inference made about Marty: _____

_____

**Apply**

Choose a word from the box below. Write a paragraph giving information about a character you invent. When making inferences about the character, the reader of your paragraph should be able to infer the word you chose. Do not use the word in your paragraph.

| clownish | loud | friendly |
|---|---|---|

_____

_____

_____

_____

_____

**COMPREHENSION**

**UNIT I** Cooperation and Competition • **Lesson 2** *The Marble Champ*

# Pronouns

| Rule | Example |
|---|---|
| ▶ A **pronoun** is used in place of one or more nouns. | ▶ John gave **John's** speech today. John gave **his** speech today. |
| ▶ When you speak of yourself and someone else, always speak of yourself last. | ▶ Bonita and **I** will help you. |

## Try It!

**Circle the pronouns in this paragraph.**

A family tree shows your relatives. A relative is a person who belongs to the same family as you. I showed my family tree in class. My mom's relatives are on the right. The left side shows relatives of my dad. I have many cousins. They are my relatives too.

**UNIT 1** Cooperation and Competition • **Lesson 2** *The Marble Champ*

## Practice

**Circle the correct word.**

1. **Mine   My**   dad and   **I   me**   made a keepsake box.

2. **Its   It's**   filled with things that mean a lot to   **us   we.**

3. **He   Him**   gave   **I   me**   a jacket of   **him   his**   from high school.

4. In the box,   **their   there**   are a lot of track medals that **he   him**   won.

5. You would like making a box like   **ours   our's.**

6. **Your   You're**   in for a treat!

## Proofread

**Write a pronoun above each underlined word.**

Some people are concerned about recycling. <u>People</u> recycle plastic, paper, and other reusable items. My brother Alberto takes plastic soda bottles to the recycling center. <u>Alberto</u> also donates his outgrown clothes to the thrift shop. <u>The thrift shop</u> sells <u>the clothes</u> for very affordable prices. The clerks at the shop are glad when Alberto visits. <u>The clerks</u> are eager to help <u>Alberto</u> carry in <u>Alberto's</u> box.

**GRAMMAR AND USAGE**

# Author's Point of View

**Focus** Writers must decide from whose **point of view** they will tell a story.

> ▶ Stories told through the eyes of a character in the story are in the **first-person point of view.** A first-person narrator uses words such as *I, me, we, us, our,* and *my.*
>
> ▶ Stories told through the eyes of an outside storyteller are in the **third-person point of view.** A third-person narrator uses words such as *he, she, him, her, them, theirs, his,* and *hers.*

## Identify

Read the following paragraph from "Juggling" and write whether it is in the first-person or third-person point of view. Then, rewrite the paragraph, changing the point of view.

**1.** In gym class on Monday, we started volleyball, and I hit seven straight serves just over the net, hard and fast. Mr. Braden called me over at the end of class.

Point of view: _____

New paragraph: _____

_____

_____

_____

_____

_____

**UNIT 1**  Cooperation and Competition • **Lesson 3** *Juggling*

▶**Author's Point of View**

### Practice and Apply

Read each paragraph and write whether it is in first-person or third-person point of view. Then rewrite the paragraph, changing the point of view.

1. When Shelly moved to a new neighborhood, she wasn't sure she liked the kids who lived there, but when she got an invitation to her next-door neighbor's birthday party, she made several new friends.

   Point of view: _____

   New paragraph: _____

   _____

   _____

   _____

   _____

2. "Never in my wildest dreams did I expect to see you here!" shouted Andy in surprise. I just stood up and smiled. It was good to see Andy after so many months.

   Point of view: _____

   New paragraph: _____

   _____

   _____

   _____

   _____

**COMPREHENSION**

# Verbs

| Rule | Example |
| --- | --- |
| ▶ An action verb tells what a person or thing is doing. | ▶ Mieko **hit** the ball out of the park. |
| ▶ State-of-being verbs show a condition of existence. | ▶ Ms. Chandler **is** here. |
| ▶ Some state-of-being verbs can be linking verbs. A linking verb tells what the person or thing is or is like. | ▶ Ms. Chandler **is** our principal. |
| ▶ An auxiliary verb helps the main verb show action or express a state of being. | ▶ We <u>have</u> **traveled** across California. They <u>are</u> **traveling** to Arizona. |

**Circle the verbs in this paragraph.**

Today, there are more than 500 Native American groups in the United States. Many people in these groups live on special areas of land, or reservations, that were reserved by the government. The largest reservation is the Navajo Reservation, which covers 16 million acres in Arizona, New Mexico, and Utah.

▶**Verbs**

**GRAMMAR AND USAGE**

## Practice

Write three sentences that tell about something that happened yesterday. Some examples are *I finished my math homework. I ate dinner. I read a book to my little sister.*

_____

_____

_____

Underline the action verbs in this paragraph. Circle the state-of-being verbs. Put brackets around the auxiliary verbs.

Alex was in the track meet yesterday after school. He won second place in the long jump. He jumped 14 feet 3 inches! He had jumped even farther than that before yesterday.

## Proofread

Write a different verb above each underlined word(s).

Just before he got ready to jump, Alex looked around the crowd for friendly faces. When he saw us, he smiled. He ran down the runway and jumped as far as he could. He looked back to where he had landed. Then he got up and came over to us. We all told Alex that he had made a great jump. He said that he could do better, and he went back to wait for his next turn.

**UNIT I** Cooperation and Competition • **Lesson 3** *Juggling*

# Figurative Language

| Rule | Example |
|---|---|
| ▶ A **simile** compares two things that are not alike by using either *like* or *as*. | ▶ The dogs leaped through the tall grass like jackrabbits. |
| ▶ A **metaphor** compares two things that are not alike without using *like* or *as*. | ▶ The dogs were jackrabbits leaping through the tall grass. |
| ▶ **Personification** gives nonhuman things or ideas qualities that are human. | ▶ The blowing leaves whirled and pirouetted in a graceful ballet. |
| ▶ **Hyperbole** is an extreme exaggeration often used for humorous effect. | ▶ My locker was clamped shut like a bank safe. |
| ▶ An **idiom** is a phrase that cannot be understood by knowing only the literal meaning. | ▶ When we heard we made the playoffs, we had baseball on the brain. |

 **List the figure of speech used in each sentence below.**

1. The pool water was so cold we expected to see an iceberg

   floating by at any moment. _____

2. When it came to chess, they were peas in a pod.

   _____

3. Wailing for attention, the solitary cat cried in the

   night. _____

4. The sea of grass stretched as far as we could see.

   _____

**UNIT I** Cooperation and Competition • **Lesson 3** *Juggling*

▶**Figurative Language**

**Practice**

**Write a sentence for each figure of speech listed. Use the ideas provided or any of your own.**

5. Write a sentence containing a simile. Ideas: *rain, the sound of a jet, the atmosphere in the hall at a specific time of day.*

_____

_____

6. Write a sentence containing a metaphor. Ideas: *your favorite animal, the approach of evening, the sounds at a construction site.*

_____

_____

7. Write a sentence that uses personification. Ideas: *a computer, a change in weather, a landscape.*

_____

_____

8. Write a sentence that uses hyperbole. Ideas: *a hot day, the result of something you made, the longest distance you walked or traveled.*

_____

_____

9. Write a sentence containing an idiom. Ideas: *stick together, for the birds, on cloud nine.*

_____

_____

**WRITER'S CRAFT**

# Sequence

**Focus** To help readers make sense of what they read, writers show the **sequence,** or order, of events by using time words and order words.

> **Time words** and **order words** provide readers with clues about which events happen before or after others in a story.
> ▶ Some words that indicate time are *yesterday, tomorrow, morning, night, moment, minute, suddenly,* and *last year.*
> ▶ Some words that indicate order are *first, last, after, next, finally,* and *then.*

## Identify

Look through "The Abacus Contest." Find examples of words or phrases used by the author to indicate a certain amount of time, a certain time of day, or the order in which events take place.

**1.** Page: _____ Paragraph: _____

Word or phrase: _____

_____

**2.** Page: _____ Paragraph: _____

Word or phrase: _____

_____

**3.** Page: _____ Paragraph: _____

Word or phrase: _____

_____

▶**Sequence**

**COMPREHENSION**

### Practice

Read each sentence. Then, fill in the blanks with a word or phrase that indicates time or order.

1. We are going to the movies, and _____ we are going out to dinner.

2. I will call my friend _____ I do my homework.

3. We waited in line impatiently, but _____ they let us in.

4. _____ I went to school, but this week is a vacation.

5. My birthday was _____.

### Apply

Write a paragraph about the things you did yesterday. Be sure to include time words and order words to help the reader understand when each event took place.

_____

_____

_____

_____

_____

_____

_____

_____

_____

# Kinds of Sentences

| Rule | Example |
|------|---------|
| ▶ A **declarative** sentence makes a statement. It always ends with a period. | ▶ My best friend is Reynaldo. |
| ▶ An **interrogative** sentence asks a question. It ends with a question mark. | ▶ Did you see the goal Ana made? |
| ▶ An **imperative** sentence gives a command or makes a request. It usually ends with a period. | ▶ Please call the police. |
| ▶ An **exclamatory** sentence expresses a strong feeling. It ends with an exclamation point. | ▶ That was a yummy dessert! |

 **Add the correct end punctuation to these sentences.**

1. Do you know anything about Alaska

2. The United States bought Alaska from Russia in 1867

3. Henry Seward was the Secretary of State at that time, and he arranged to purchase Alaska for $7 million

4. People called the territory "Seward's Folly" because they thought it cost too much money

5. An amazing thing happened five years later

6. The discovery of gold started a rush to Alaska

7. Can you name two important energy sources also found there

**Kinds of Sentences**

## Practice

**Add punctuation to separate the paragraph into sentences. Underline the first word in each new sentence.**

Three quarters of the world's freshwater is frozen much of it is in glaciers, huge masses of ice that move across the land water is also frozen in large masses of floating ice called icebergs what an amazing sight icebergs must be would you please find a picture of an iceberg to add to your report bring it in tomorrow.

## Proofread

**Correct the punctuation in this paragraph. Draw three lines under letters that should be capitalized at the beginnings of sentences.**

One of America's most important artists is Georgia O'Keeffe? she is famous for her paintings of natural objects such as rocks, bones, and clouds. have you ever seen her painting of a red gladiola! what talent she had to show exactly what she saw in each blossom I wonder how she did that? O'Keeffe used the red hills near her ranch in New Mexico as the setting for many of her paintings.

**GRAMMAR AND USAGE**

Name _____  Date _____

# Sensory Description

Sensory detail describes look, sound, feel, smell, and taste. By engaging the readers' senses, sensory description helps them imagine that they are sharing the experience.

| **Rule** | **Example** |
|---|---|
| ▶ It uses **sight** to create detailed visual pictures. | ▶ The tide had softened the footprints and holes made earlier in the sand so they appeared as gentle impressions. |
| ▶ It uses **sound** to engage the reader's sense of hearing. | ▶ Only when everything was quiet did we notice the steady hum of the refrigerator. |
| ▶ It uses **touch** to re-create how something feels. | ▶ The wet, gritty sand scratched my head and clung to my eyelashes. |
| ▶ It uses **smell** to create a mental image of how something smells. | ▶ The odor of burnt popcorn hung in the air. |
| ▶ It uses **taste** to appeal to the reader's sense of taste. | ▶ The sweet, creamy ice cream dissolved in our mouths. |

 **Try It!** **Write which of the five senses each sentence describes.**

1. The sweet, slightly bitter aroma of cocoa from the

   chocolate factory drifted toward us. _____

2. Our dog's nails click when she runs across the floor. _____

3. A layer of steam covered my glasses. _____

4. I ran my tongue over the raw, bare spot left by my

   missing tooth. _____

5. Its sourness made us pucker. _____

**UNIT I** Cooperation and Competition • **Lesson 4** *The Abacus Contest*

▶ **Sensory Description**

## Practice

Go to or imagine being in a place where you can soak up and describe sensory detail. It may be your desk, the playground, the gym, the hallway, or another place rich in sensation. Next, write a description of that place using each of the senses.

**6.** Sight _____

**7.** Hearing _____

**8.** Touch _____

**9.** Smell _____

**10.** Taste _____

**Descriptive paragraphs often provide readers with more than one sensory detail. List the sensory details and the related senses used in this paragraph.**

**11.** The pungent odor of cranberries filled the air in my grandmother's kitchen. She always made fresh cranberry sauce for the holidays. This year I promised her I would at least try a taste. She smiled as she handed me a bright red spoonful. I made a face, and the sound of my grandma's laughter rang throughout the kitchen. I forced myself to take a bite. I was surprised by the tangy sweetness of the lumpy berries.

_____

_____

_____

_____

**WRITER'S CRAFT**

# Compare and Contrast

**Focus** Writers often use **comparison** and **contrast** to help readers understand ideas.

> To **compare** means to tell how two or more things are similar, or alike. Some words that signal comparison are *both*, *like*, *as*, *also*, *too*, and *neither . . . nor*.
>
> To **contrast** means to tell how two or more things are different. Some words that signal contrast are *different*, *instead of*, *but*, *rather than*, and *unlike*.

## Identify

Find two sentences in "S.O.R. Losers" that contain comparisons or contrasts. Write their page and paragraph numbers along with the sentences. Then, identify the two or more things being compared or contrasted.

**1.** Page: _____     Paragraph: _____

Sentence: _____

_____

Comparison or Contrast: _____

_____

**2.** Page: _____     Paragraph: _____

Sentence: _____

_____

Comparison or Contrast: _____

_____

**UNIT I** Cooperation and Competition • **Lesson 5** *S.O.R. Losers*

▶**Compare and Contrast**

### Practice

Combine each pair of sentences into one sentence that compares or contrasts. Use clue words to make the meaning clear.

1. Cars are not allowed in the park. Bicycles are allowed in the park.

   _____

   _____

2. The dolphins put on an excellent performance. The seals forgot their tricks.

   _____

   _____

3. My family loves dogs. Max's family loves dogs.

   _____

   _____

### Apply

Write a sentence comparing two movies that you've seen or two songs that you've heard. Then, write a sentence contrasting them.

1. Comparison: _____

   _____

2. Contrast: _____

   _____

COMPREHENSION

# Subjects and Predicates

| Rule | Example |
|---|---|
| ▶ The **subject** is the part of the sentence that tells *who* or *what*. A **simple subject** does not have any other words that describe the subject. A **complete subject** is the subject and all the words that describe it. | simple subject<br>▶ My cousin Elizabeth got a new car.<br>complete subject |
| ▶ The **predicate** is the part of the sentence that describes or tells what the subject does. A **simple predicate** is always the main verb in the sentence. A **complete predicate** is the main verb and all the words that tell something about it. | simple predicate<br>▶ Elizabeth got a new car.<br>complete predicate |
| ▶ All sentences need a subject and a predicate. Without a subject or predicate, a sentence becomes a **fragment**. | ▶ Scratched Elizabeth's new car. (missing subject)<br>A scratch in Elizabeth's new car. (missing predicate) |

 **Try It!** **Circle the simple subject and underline the simple predicate in each sentence.**

A natural resource is a material found in nature that is useful or necessary to living things. Some natural resources are water, oxygen, soil, trees, and minerals.

Some natural resources are renewable. A renewable resource can be replaced in about 30 years. People need and use a lot of renewable resources. For example, freshwater is necessary for people to live. People also use wood from trees for many products.

**UNIT I**  Cooperation and Competition • **Lesson 5** *S.O.R. Losers*

## ▶ Subjects and Predicates

### Practice

**Circle the complete subject and underline the complete predicate in each sentence.**

The Nile River is the longest river on Earth. It flows through the northeastern part of Africa. One of the countries it flows through is Egypt. The Nile has had a big effect on life in Egypt.

A kind of flat-bottomed sailboat called a felucca has been traveling on the Nile for thousands of years. Feluccas carry passengers and goods. Travelers on feluccas see deserts with herds of camels and, as the Nile gets closer to the Mediterranean Sea, green, fertile farmlands.

### Proofread

**Circle the fragments in the following paragraph.**

The Lakota did not build permanent villages. The Lakota lived in teepees. Made of poles and animal hides. When the Lakota wanted to move. They carried their belongings on wood frames tied to their horses. In order to follow the buffalo herds. The hunters tried to frighten the animals into a circle.

GRAMMAR AND USAGE

**UNIT I**   Cooperation and Competition • **Lesson 5** *S.O.R. Losers*

# Time and Order Words

| **Rule** | **Example** |
|---|---|
| ▶ Describe the **time** when events happen by using transition words such as *yesterday, this morning, this afternoon,* and *today.* | ▶ Two days ago I found out about the math test. I studied yesterday, took the test today, and will find out how I did tomorrow. |
| ▶ When you organize by **order of occurrence,** you tell when events occur in relationship to one another. Use transition words such as *before, first, next, then, later,* and *last.* | ▶ First, I will brainstorm for ideas. Next, I will plan how to research and present an idea. After I write my rough draft, I'll revise it. Then I will proofread my writing and, last, get it ready to publish. |
| ▶ When you organize by **order of importance,** you arrange reasons from **least** to **most** important for persuasive writing. Organize information in news stories from **most** to **least** important. Use words such as *first, most important,* and *finally.* | ▶ (School newspaper) The Sandhill band won first place at the district competition. They had been practicing "Stars and Stripes Forever" for six months. The last time the Sandhill band won at districts was in 1998. |

**For each paragraph, list the method used to organize the information.**

1. Before I run in a race, I warm up. First I stretch my muscles. Next I walk around to loosen up and relax. Then I take off my sweats and position myself by the starting

   blocks. _____

2. Everybody at Sandhill School should come to cheer on the girl's field hockey team. First, field hockey is an exciting sport to watch. Second, cheering on the team is good for school spirit. Last, the girls need everybody's support.

_____

**Time and Order Words**

**Practice**

3. Write a short paragraph about how you put together a
   project. Organize your information by *time*.

   _____

   _____

   _____

   _____

4. Write a short paragraph about getting ready for school.
   Organize your information by *order of occurrence*.

   _____

   _____

   _____

   _____

5. Write the beginning paragraph for a news story about
   something that happened at your school. Organize
   information by *order of importance*.

   _____

   _____

   _____

**WRITER'S CRAFT**

# Author's Purpose

**Focus** Writers always have a **purpose** for writing a story.

> The author's reason for writing a story is called the **author's purpose.**
> ▶ The author's purpose can be to inform, explain, entertain, or persuade. An author can have more than one purpose for writing.
> ▶ The author's purpose affects the details, descriptions, pictures, and dialogue that are included in a story.

## Identify

Read "Founders of the Children's Rain Forest" and then answer the following questions.

1. What do you think the author's main purpose or purposes were for writing this selection?

   _____

2. What makes you think this was the purpose?

   _____

   _____

   _____

   _____

3. How successful do you think the author was in this purpose?

   _____

   _____

   _____

**UNIT 1**  Cooperation and Competition • **Lesson 6**  *Founders of the Children's Rain Forest*

▶ **Author's Purpose**

## Practice

Read the following paragraphs and write the author's purpose for each.

**1.** The story "Alice in Wonderland" was originally written by Lewis Carroll as a gift for a young child named Alice. The story included his own illustrations. These were very different from any of the illustrations that were done later when he expanded the story into a book-length version.

Author's purpose: _____

**2.** I invented a new game. You need four bases, in-line skates for all players, a soccer ball, and a bat. First, set up the bases as you would in baseball—first, second, third, and home. Then, have a pitcher throw the soccer ball to the batter. The batter tries to hit the ball with the bat. As in baseball, the batter has three strikes before he or she is out. If the batter is successful, he or she skates around the bases. Doesn't it sound like fun?

Author's purpose: _____

## Apply

Take some factual information that you know or have heard in the news and use it to write an opening paragraph for an entertaining story.

_____

_____

_____

_____

_____

_____

COMPREHENSION

# Review

## Nouns

**Write the plural form of each noun.**

1. woman       _____

2. mouse       _____

3. country      _____

## Pronouns

**Circle the pronouns in this paragraph.**

A Pilgrim described Chief Massasoit as follows: "In his attire he was little or nothing differing from the rest of his followers. . . . and he oiled both head and face. . . . All his followers likewise were in their faces, in part or in whole, painted."

## Verbs

**Underline the action verbs in this paragraph. Write a different verb above each word(s) you underlined. Put brackets around the auxiliary verbs.**

Jeff looked up at the night sky. First he saw the Big Dipper, then he saw Sirius, the Dog Star. Finally he saw the planet Venus. While he was looking at the sky, he saw a shooting star. Jeff knew that it was not really a star but a meteor. He had learned that in science class last year. The last thing he saw was a huge airplane. Its bright red and green lights flashed brightly in the clear night sky.

## Kinds of Sentences

▶ **Review**

**Correct the punctuation in this paragraph. Draw three lines under letters that should be capitalized.**

Do you know what a jury is. a jury is a group of people chosen to decide the truth from the evidence given in a court of law? the 12 people on the jury must be fair and impartial! lawyers call witnesses to testify and answer questions about the facts of the case. then the jury leaves the courtroom to discuss the issue until they reach an agreement on the verdict? what an awesome responsibility it is to be on a jury?

## Subjects and Predicates

**Write *yes* before each group of words that is a sentence. Write *no* for the other groups.**

4. _____ Newspapers keep everyone in touch with local and world events.

5. _____ And all for a few cents a day.

6. _____ Stories in the paper cover a wide range of topics.

7. _____ Also information about the arts, technology, and the environment.

8. _____ A special type style that sets it apart from others.

9. _____ Some try to remain independent.

10. _____ Has a large staff of reporters, cartoonists, and typesetters.

**GRAMMAR AND USAGE**

# Presentation

> **Presentation** refers to the look of a piece of writing. Writers will often add charts, graphs, bullets, illustrations, italics, or other effects to make their writing more visually appealing.
>
> **Before**
> ▶ There are 11 boys and 10 girls in my class.
>
> **Improved**
> ▶ There are 11 boys and 10 girls in my class.
>
>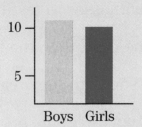
>
> ▶ Chasmosaurus was a dinosaur that looked like a rhinoceros. Another dinosaur, the Styracosaurus, had six spikes on its head.
> ▶ Some other dinosaurs include Coelophysis, Iguanodon, Parasaurolophus,and Vulcanodon.
>
> ▶ **Chasmosaurus** was a dinosaur that looked like a rhinoceros. Another dinosaur, the **Styracosaurus,** had six spikes on its head.
> ▶ Some other dinosaurs are
>   • Coelophysis
>   • Iguanodon
>   • Parasaurolophus
>   • Vulcanodon

 **Write what type of graphic you might use to make the sentence more visually appealing.**

1. Some things I might need for revising include a dictionary, a thesaurus, and a pencil.

_____

2. Half of the class voted to go to the zoo, one quarter chose the science center, and one quarter picked the history

   museum. _____

**UNIT 1**  Cooperation and Competition • **Lesson 6**  *Founders of the Children's Rain Forest*

### Practice

**Draw a chart or graph to include with the following paragraph to make it more visually appealing.**

**3.** The five tallest mountains in North America are Mt. McKinley at 20,320 feet; Mt. St. Elias at 18,008 feet; Mt. Foraker at 17,400 feet; Mt. Bona at 16,500 feet; and Mt. Blackburn at 16,390 feet.

**Create a time line to help illustrate these facts.**

**4.** Alaska was purchased from Russia in 1861 for 7.2 million dollars. In 1948, the Alaska Highway was opened for public travel. Alaska became the 49th state in 1959. On March 27, 1964, the strongest earthquake recorded in North America hit Alaska. In 1989, a ship spilled 11 million gallons of oil into Prince William Sound. The state population reached 550,000 in 1990.

**WRITER'S CRAFT**

**UNIT 2** **Back Through the Stars • Lesson I** *Galileo*

# Capitalization: Places

| Rule | Example |
|---|---|
| ▶ Capitalize the names of countries, cities, states, counties, bodies of water, mountains, and other place names. | ▶ India<br>New York City<br>the Swiss Alps |
| ▶ Capitalize the names of months and days. | ▶ February<br>Friday |
| ▶ Capitalize the names of holidays. | ▶ New Year's Day |
| ▶ Capitalize people's titles. | ▶ Senator Bill Harding<br>President Lincoln |

**Circle the words that should begin with a capital letter.**

1. In columbus, ohio, there is a celebration on columbus day.

2. Is there a fourth of july in england?

3. In our city, we plant trees on arbor day.

4. We honor president washington on the third monday in february.

5. On july 1, canada celebrates its independence.

6. In mexico, independence is celebrated on september 15 and 16.

7. Our nation's leaders declared that thanksgiving day would be the fourth thursday in november.

**UNIT 2** Back Through the Stars • **Lesson 1** *Galileo*

**▶Capitalization: Places**

## Practice

**Draw three lines under letters that should be capitalized.**

Some holidays are celebrated just for fun. On valentine's day, february 14, we send special cards to people we love. We honor mothers on mother's day, the second sunday in may; and fathers on father's day, the third sunday in june. I think we should have a children's day, as japan does!

## Proofread

**Draw three lines under letters that should be capital letters. Draw a slash through letters that should be small letters.**

Some Holidays honor american heroes. The First president, george Washington, explorer Christopher columbus, and civil rights Leader Martin luther king jr. are all remembered with Public Holidays. On memorial day, america remembers those who died in Wars. We celebrate the men and women who served in the armed forces on veterans day. On labor day, we don't work because we are celebrating working people!

**MECHANICS**

**UNIT 2** **Back Through the Stars • Lesson 1** *Galileo*

# Organizing by Order

To make descriptions and explanations clear, order information by *time, order of occurrence,* or *order of importance.*

**Rule**

▶ Describe the **time** when events happen from most to least recent or from least to most recent. Use transition words such as *yesterday, this morning, this afternoon, today,* and *tomorrow.*

▶ Use **order of occurrence** to organize by telling when events occur in relationship to one another. Use transition words such as *before, first, next, then, later,* and *last.*

▶ To organize writing by **order of importance,** order information from least to most important for persuasive writing and from most to least important for news writing.

**Example**

▶ Tomorrow I will add the final coat of finish to my dinosaur model. Today I applied the first and second coats of paint. Yesterday I built the model.

▶ Before serving the frozen yogurt, let it thaw for five minutes. Then dip the scoop in water and begin to scoop. Last, add a cookie to each dish and serve.

▶ Everybody in our class should read *Treasure Island.* First, it is a good example of an adventure story. Second, it is a highly entertaining book. Third and most important, it is assigned, and we will be tested on it Friday.

 **Try It!** **Write how each of these descriptions should be organized, by *time, order of occurrence,* or *order of importance.***

1. Instructions on how to write a friendly letter. _____

2. A day-by-day description of an across-the-globe sailboat race.

   _____

3. A persuasive paragraph on the importance of stretching one's

   muscles before running. _____

**Organizing by Order**

WRITER'S CRAFT

## Practice

**Organize information and tell how you ordered it—by**
*time, order of occurrence, order of importance (news)*
**or** *order of importance (persuasive).*

**4.** Write a short description telling how to make your favorite
food.

_____

_____

_____

**5.** Write a short paragraph describing a newsworthy event at
your school.

_____

_____

_____

**6.** Write a short paragraph giving reasons either for or against
holding a backwards day at school.

_____

_____

_____

**7.** Write a short description of how you celebrated your last
three birthdays.

_____

_____

_____

**UNIT 2** Back Through the Stars • **Lesson 1** *Galileo*

# Place and Location Words

Place and location transition words help describe places, scenes, large physical objects, and even people. Order the details so they are easy to follow and invite readers to picture what is being described.

| **Rule** | **Example** |
|---|---|
| ▶ Place and location transition words point readers in the right direction. | ▶ *above, across, around, beside, behind, inside, nearby, outside, under* |
| ▶ Some transition words form two or more word phrases. | ▶ *on top of, in back of, in front of, to the far right, to the left, to the rear* |
| ▶ Place and location transition words may organize descriptions from top to bottom or from left to right (rarely the other way around). | ▶ To the far left of the lifeguard stand we saw the sand scooters. To the right of the scooters were the beach chairs and cabanas. To the right of them were the lifeboat and life buoys. |

**Circle the place and location transition words used in this description and write how it is organized.**

1. A small propeller spun from the top of his baseball cap. Brown straight hair stuck out from under the cap in all directions. Under his long bangs, blue eyes peered out. At the bottom of his neck, we saw his green and orange polka dotted tie. Beneath that he wore a maroon shirt.

Organization: _____

**UNIT 2**   Back Through the Stars • **Lesson 1** *Galileo*

▶ **Place and Location Words**

### Practice

Keep in mind that place and location description words may also describe from inside to outside, far to near, near to far, or any other way that makes sense for what is being described.

Use place and location transition words to describe each of the following. Tell how you organized each description by filling in the spaces.

**2.** Describe a wide billboard. _____

_____

_____

Organized from _____ to _____.

**3.** Describe a watermelon from outer skin to inner pulp.

_____

_____

Organized from _____ to _____.

**4.** Describe a school locker. _____

_____

_____

Organized from _____ to _____.

**5.** Describe what you might see looking out over a lake,

beginning with what is near. _____

_____

_____

Organized from _____ to _____.

**WRITER'S CRAFT**

# Capitalization: Titles

| Rule | Example |
|---|---|
| ▶ Capitalize proper adjectives that come from proper nouns. | ▶ French bread, Swiss watch |
| ▶ Titles of books, movies, magazines, and newspapers are capitalized. | ▶ *Charlotte's Web*<br>*The Parent Trap*<br>*National Geographic*<br>*San Francisco Examiner* |
| ▶ Capitalize the names of historic events. | ▶ the Civil War<br>the Boston Tea Party |
| ▶ Capitalize the names of religions, languages, and ethnic backgrounds. | ▶ Islam<br>Greek<br>Latino |

 **Try It!**   **Rewrite each example with the proper capitalization.**

1. Our new puppy is an english setter. _____

2. rocky mountain sheep _____

3. I have a copy of *and then there were none* written in

   german. _____

4. Did Jack London write *call of the wild?*

   _____

5. Our assignment is to read the *gettysburg address.*

   _____

6. world war II _____

7. my spanish class _____

▶ **Capitalization: Titles**

**Practice**

**Draw three lines under letters that should be capitalized.**

*The astronomer* and *astronomy now* are popular british magazines. Readers can learn about everything from stars and planets to telescopes and other instruments used to gaze at the heavens. It was greek and arab scholars who first looked to the sky and tried to understand the moon, stars, and planets. It was not until the invention of the telescope in the seventeenth century that they got a clear picture of the heavens. The first planet discovered in the milky way galaxy was Uranus, in 1781, by the english astronomer William Herschel. An american astronomer, Clyde Tombaugh, discovered Pluto in 1930.

**Proofread**

**Draw three lines under letters that should be capital letters. Draw a slash through letters that should be small letters.**

In the Third Century B.C., the greek scientist Aristarchus suggested that Earth and the Planets move around the Sun. The Telescope, first used to observe the skies by the italian scientist Galileo, proved this to be true. Since then, Astronomers have used telescopes to explore into the farthest parts of our Solar System and beyond. For example, the hubble Space telescope is an optic telescope that flies high above Earth.

**MECHANICS**

# Compare and Contrast

Compare and contrast subjects in your writing to create clearer pictures for readers. When you compare and contrast, you emphasize the differences and similarities of what you are writing about.

| **Rule** | **Example** |
|---|---|
| ▶ To compare means to tell how things, events, or characters are similar, or alike. Use signal words such as *both*, *same*, *like*, *as*, *also*, and *too*. | ▶ Both Jake and Elaine liked to read mysteries. |
| ▶ To contrast means to tell how things, events, or characters are different. Use signal words such as *different*, *but*, *unlike*, *than*, *in contrast*, and *although*. | ▶ Jake likes mystery movies, but Elaine does not. |
| ▶ Some things may be both compared and contrasted. | ▶ In both the book and the movie, Jerome solves the mystery, but only the book tells how Lauren helped him. |

 **Try It!** **Write a sentence or two comparing, contrasting, or comparing and contrasting the following.**

**1.** Compare a large lake and an ocean.

_____

**2.** Contrast a Monday and a Saturday.

_____

**3.** Compare and contrast riding on a bus and riding in a car.

_____

▶**Compare and Contrast**

**WRITER'S CRAFT**

**Practice**

**Read each sentence and tell whether it compares or contrasts. Then rewrite each sentence the opposite way. Note the change that occurs in the meaning.**

**4.** Dave and Edmund both finished all their vegetables.

_____

_____

**5.** Marta plays the trombone, while Janet plays the cello.

_____

_____

**6.** I like to write poetry just like my sister Gina.

_____

_____

**7.** Both cats and dogs make good pets.

_____

_____

**Write a paragraph comparing or contrasting yourself to a family member. Be sure to include the ways that you are similar and the ways that you are different.**

**8.** _____

_____

_____

_____

_____

# Abbreviations

| Rule | Example |
|---|---|
| ▶ Most abbreviations are formed with periods. | ▶ p.m.<br>Jr.<br>blvd.<br>mph |
| ▶ Only one period is used if an abbreviation comes at the end of a sentence. | ▶ School is over at 3 p.m. |
| ▶ Capitalize abbreviations of proper nouns and titles used before names. | ▶ U.S.A.<br>Gen. Palmer |

**Circle the abbreviations that should be capitalized.**
**Place periods where needed.**

**1.** I voted for sen White in November.

**2.** Are mr and mrs Armstrong related to the astronaut?

**3.** Didn't e b White write *Charlotte's Web*?

**4.** Isn't it true that www stands for World Wide Web?

**5.** The recipe says to add 1 pt of sour cream.

**6.** Please introduce u s rep Hargrove before her speech.

**UNIT 2**   Back Through the Stars • **Lesson 3**  *The Heavenly Zoo*

 **Abbreviations**

## Practice

**Write the abbreviations of the following words.**

7. Sunday                     _____

8. Tuesday                   _____

9. Thursday                 _____

10. Saturday                _____

11. January                  _____

12. September             _____

13. Doctor                    _____

14. Mister                    _____

15. for your information  _____

16. ounce                    _____

17. teaspoon               _____

18. inch                       _____

## Proofread

**Draw three lines under letters that should be capital letters. Place periods where needed.**

My brother Samuel would like to go to st John's College in Annapolis, md. We went there in feb to tour the campus. It is near Washington, d c.

We learned that st John's was founded in 1784. Its charter is said to have been written by the rev William Smith. Four of the college founders had signed the Declaration of Independence. St John's is famous for having students study classical world literature to learn all subjects.

**MECHANICS**

# Aim/Purpose/Audience

| **Rule** | **Example** |
|---|---|
| ▶ **Aim** is your specific goal, focus, or reason for writing. | ▶ You write a persuasive report on protecting horseshoe crabs in the Delaware Bay. Your aim is to convince readers to help protect the crabs. |
| ▶ **Purpose** is *why* you are writing. It may be to inform, to explain, to entertain, or to persuade. | ▶ You write a fantasy story about two talking horseshoe crabs who make a trip across the Delaware Bay. Your purpose is to entertain. |
| ▶ **Audience** refers to your readers. The information and language you use should appeal to their interests, experience, and level of understanding. | ▶ You use simple yet lively language for a story about talking horseshoe crabs because your audience is 5–8 year olds. |

 **Read the paragraphs below and write the author's purpose for each one.**

1. To grow tomatoes, first plant the seeds in soil in small starter pots. Water the pots and set them in a sunny place. Within a few days, you should see the seedlings coming up. Be sure to keep the seedlings moist. When the seedlings are about a foot high, plant them outside. Water the plants immediately.

   Author's purpose: _____

2. Tomatoes are one of the most popular items in the produce section of the grocery store. Although most people think tomatoes are vegetables, they are actually fruits. In the early 1500s, tomatoes were thought to be poisonous.

   Author's purpose: _____

**UNIT 2** Back Through the Stars • **Lesson 3** *The Heavenly Zoo*

▶ **Aim/Purpose/Audience**

**Practice**

**Write what you think would be the aim, purpose, and audience for these writing suggestions.**

**3.** A story about a runaway kite and the adventure two kids have trying to catch it.

Aim: _____

Purpose: _____

Audience: _____

**4.** An article telling how to fly a kite in a school newsletter.

Aim: _____

Purpose: _____

Audience: _____

**5.** A poster at the supermarket encouraging people to participate in the local kite festival.

Aim: _____

Purpose: _____

Audience: _____

**6.** A school report on the history of the box kite.

Aim: _____

Purpose: _____

Audience: _____

**WRITER'S CRAFT**

# Main Idea and Details

**Focus** Authors organize their writing into **main ideas** supported by **details.**

> The **main idea** is what the text is about.
> ▶ A main idea should be clear and focused.
> ▶ A main idea should have supporting details.
> **Details** provide additional information about the main idea.

## Identify

Read "Circles, Squares, and Daggers: How Native Americans Watched the Skies" and complete the following exercises.

**1.** What is the main idea of the entire selection?

_____

_____

**2.** Write three detail sentences that support the main idea.

Sentence 1: _____

_____

Sentence 2: _____

_____

Sentence 3: _____

_____

▶ **Main Idea and Details**

**Practice and Apply**

Write a paragraph for each of the two topic sentences
provided below. Use sentences for each paragraph
that support the main idea stated in the topic sentence.

Topic 1. sentence: Astronomy has changed drastically from the
ancient times to now.

_____

_____

_____

_____

_____

_____

Topic 2. sentence: Native Americans were able to gather information
from the skies even without the use of modern
technology.

_____

_____

_____

_____

_____

_____

**COMPREHENSION**

# Commas in Places and Dates

| Rule | Example |
|---|---|
| ▶ Use one comma to separate the name of a city from the name of its state or country and another comma to separate the name of the state or country from the rest of the sentence. | ▶ We visited Portland, Oregon, last spring. Moscow, Russia, is one of my favorite cities. |
| ▶ Do not use a comma after the state if it is followed by a ZIP code. | ▶ The bank is located at 1340 W. Franklin St., Friendswood, Texas 77546. |
| ▶ Use a comma to separate the name of a day from the name of a month. | ▶ My sister was married on Saturday, October 21. |
| ▶ Use one comma to separate the day of a month from the year and another comma to separate the year from the rest of the sentence. Do not use a comma if only the month and the year are given. | ▶ June 11, 2001, was our end-of-school party. |

**Add commas where needed in the following sentences.**

1. Neil Armstrong first set foot on the moon on July 20 1969.

2. The Boy Scouts of America was founded in February 1910.

3. The home of Elvis Presley is Graceland Memphis Tennessee.

4. Montpelier Vermont population 7,800 is a beautiful city.

**UNIT 2** Back Through the Stars • **Lesson 4** *Circles, Squares, and Daggers*

▶**Commas in Places and Dates**

### Practice

**Rewrite the heading and inside address, adding commas where needed.**

40 East Oak St. _____

San Francisco CA 94892 _____

April 25 2001 _____

Mr. Ethan Olson _____

American Museum of Art _____

704 Drummer Avenue _____

Newport Connecticut 20734 _____

### Proofread

**Correct the punctuation in this paragraph. Insert commas where they are needed, and cross them out where they are not needed.**

   On September 1 1939 Germany invaded Poland. Britain and France declared war on Germany two days later, on September 3 1939. In June, 1940, the German army entered Paris France.

   Japanese planes attacked Pearl Harbor in Honolulu Hawaii on December 7 1941. The United States, Britain, and Canada then declared war on Japan.

   In November, 1942, the British defeated Germany at El Alamein Egypt and on September 2 1945 Japan surrendered. This ended World War II.

   For more information on World War II, visit the Smithsonian Institution Washington D.C. 20560.

**MECHANICS**

# Supporting Details

When you write, support your ideas by providing **evidence—facts, examples, reasons,** and **important details.**

| **Rule** | **Example** |
|---|---|
| ▶ Include important facts to reinforce your ideas. | ▶ Penguins have inner and outer layers of feathers to keep out cold air and to prevent frostbite. |
| ▶ Include examples to make ideas easier to understand. | ▶ For example, the protective feathers of Emperor and Adelie penguins allow them to live all year in Antarctica, the coldest continent in the world. |
| ▶ Include reasons to tell why something is the way it is or why people feel a certain way. A **cause** is a type of reason that tells what makes something happen. | ▶ Penguins are very fast swimmers. Because of their great speed, penguins are usually able to escape their natural predators. |
| ▶ Include important details to make characters and settings seem real in fiction writing and more interesting in narrative nonfiction. | ▶ When Meg stepped off the plane onto the Antarctic continent, her down jacket had all the warmth of a cotton shirt. |

 **Underline the supporting details that you see in this paragraph. In the margin near each underlined item, list the type it is: fact, example, or reason.**

1. Jupiter rotates very fast. A day on Jupiter lasts only ten hours. This rapid rotation causes the clouds to be pulled out into a series of colored bands. Different substances in the clouds give them their varied colors.

## Practice

2. Write a sentence using a fact to describe a particular school rule.

_____

_____

3. Write a sentence using a reason to explain the cause or outcome of not following a school rule.

_____

_____

4. Write a sentence that includes an important detail about what a character is thinking when he or she is about to break a rule.

_____

_____

5. Write a short paragraph about a time that you were late for something. Include a fact and a reason.

_____

_____

6. Write a short paragraph describing the setting for a make-believe race. Include important details to make the scene seem real.

_____

_____

**WRITER'S CRAFT**

# Parentheses, Hyphens, Dashes, and Ellipses

| **Rule** | **Example** |
| --- | --- |
| ▶ Use parentheses to set off words that add information to or define a word in a sentence. | ▶ Enter through the back door (on the right side of the driveway). |
| ▶ Use a hyphen to create an adjective from two words that come before a noun. Hyphens are also used to divide a word between syllables when a word is broken up at the end of a line of text. | ▶ The ten-year plan is well underway. |
| ▶ Use a dash to show a sudden break in thought or speech. | ▶ Could you call my teacher—you remember her—and tell her I'm late? |
| ▶ Ellipses are three periods used to show that something has been left out, especially in a quote. Ellipses may be used at the beginning, middle, or end of a quote. | ▶ Voting . . . is your right.

▶ My hope is that you achieve great things . . . |

**Insert hyphens, parentheses, and dashes where needed in the following paragraph.**

Pitch the highness or lowness of a sound depends on the frequency of the waves coming from the object making the sound. Fast vibrations make high pitched sounds, and slow vibrations make low pitched sounds. Frequency is measured in hertz Hz. Sounds higher than 20,000 Hz people can't hear them are ultrasonic.

**UNIT 2** **Back Through the Stars • Lesson 5** *The Mystery of Mars*

▶ **Parentheses, Hyphens, Dashes, and Ellipses**

**Practice**

**Insert the correct punctuation where needed.**

Part of the Declaration of Independence says, "We hold these truths the pursuit of Happiness." Some people say that Thomas Jefferson substituted the word *estate* property for the word *happiness.* The Declaration of Independence says that government gets its power "from the consent of the governed" the people. Our founding fathers established a voter led government more than 200 years ago.

**Proofread**

**Correct the errors in the use of parentheses, hyphens, and dashes in the following paragraph.**

The ancient Egyptians developed a system of writing that was all their own hieroglyphics. This system was made of about 800 symbols, you could call them picture signs, that stood for objects or sounds. Scribes writers who kept records of details traveled throughout Egypt recording government business. One author says that because so few people back then knew how to write, "scribes were highly respected in Egypt." It was a well: deserved honor to be a scribe.

**MECHANICS**

# Taking Notes

**Rule**

▶ Use separate pages or note cards for each of your subtopics.

▶ Use a different heading for each type of information and to make going back to your notes easy.

▶ Use your own words to sum up ideas found in sources. To work quickly, abbreviate words, but write clearly to understand what you've written.

▶ Use quotation marks for exact quotes from sources and record the author's name, the publication title, and the page number.

▶ Focus only on the information that has to do with your topic. Try not to get distracted by unrelated information.

 **Try It!**

1. **Cross out the headings that would *not* be useful for organizing notes on the history of downhill skiing.**

Where downhill skiing started
How the first skis were made
Water skiing on rivers
Slalom skiing introduced as an Olympic event
Who invented snowboarding
Famous downhill skiers of the last 100 years

2. **Cross out the headings that would not be useful for organizing notes on the social roles of bees.**

Worker bees
Bee colonies
Native flowers
Queen bees
Treating bee stings

**UNIT 2** **Back Through the Stars • Lesson 5** *The Mystery of Mars*

## Practice

**Match each heading to its research note for a report on renewable energy sources.**

**Headings**                          **Research Information**

_____ **3.** Solar power        **a.** People use solar panels to collect the sun's rays for heating.

_____ **4.** Ocean water       **b.** More and more countries use wind turbines to produce energy.

_____ **5.** The wind            **c.** Generators driven by ocean waves and tides create electricity.

**Research information should always be written in your own words. Rewrite the following research information with headings. Be creative and original, adding your own information if it is factual.**

**6.** At one time, perhaps sixty or seventy million buffalo had roamed the plains. By the early 1880s, the endless herds had been wiped out. Only a few hundred buffalo were still hiding out in remote mountain valleys.

Heading: _____

_____

WRITER'S CRAFT

**UNIT 2** Back Through the Stars • **Lesson 5** *The Mystery of Mars*

# Bibliography/Citations

| **Rule** | **Example** |
|---|---|
| ▶ List entries in alphabetical order by the author's last name. If a last name is not provided, list the source alphabetically by its title. | |
| ▶ For books, list the author's full name, last name first. A comma goes after the last name and a period follows the middle name or initial (or first name if no middle name is given). Underline or italicize the title and follow it with a period. Place a comma after the publisher name and a period after the publication date. | ▶ Holmes, Kevin J. Penguins. Bridgestone Books, 1998. |
| ▶ For magazines include the author's name (last name first), title of the article in quotation marks, the title of the magazine (with month, day, and year), and also the page numbers of the article. | ▶ Cox, Ellen T. "Women Spies of Revolution." Jr. Historian 7 May 2001: 5–15. |
| ▶ For encyclopedias include the article title, reference book title, and year published. | ▶ "Solar Energy." The World Book Encyclopedia. 2001 ed. |

 **Try It!** Read each bibliographic entry below and determine by its format which type of source it is. Write *book*, *magazine*, *encyclopedia*, or *video* in the space.

**1.** Diaz, Brett R. "Cannonball Clues." Civil War Sleuth 8 June

2000: 9–17. Type: _____

**2.** Clark, John  R. Snorkeling: A Complete Guide to the Underwater Experience. Prentice Hall, Inc., 1985.

Type: _____

**UNIT 2**  Back Through the Stars • **Lesson 5** *The Mystery of Mars*

▶ **Bibliography/Citations**

**Practice**

**The bibliographic entries below are incorrectly formatted and punctuated. Rewrite each correctly on the lines provided. Refer to the rule box for help.**

**3.** Jacob T., Horwitz, <u>The Art of Mosaics</u> 2002: Pennsylvania Press.

_____

_____

**4.** "Seeing in the Dark: How Nocturnal Animals See at Night" by Siri Lin, "Trailblazer Magazine." October, 1999, pages 34–39.

_____

_____

**5.** List three bibliographic entries in alphabetical order. Try to use more than one type of citation. Use the correct formatting and punctuation for each.

_____

_____

_____

_____

_____

_____

**WRITER'S CRAFT**

# Classifying and Categorizing

**Focus** When readers put things or ideas into groups based on shared characteristics, it helps them organize their thoughts and remember the different kinds of details in a story.

> **Classify** means to put similar things together into a group, or category. **Categories** are the actual groups that similar things are put into.
> ▶ Objects, characters, and events can often fit into more than one category.
> ▶ A broad category can often be broken into more specific categories.

## Identify

Look through the first two pages of "Stars" and list five classifications of heavenly bodies found in the sky.

1. _____

2. _____

3. _____

4. _____

5. _____

Comprehension and Language Arts Skills

**UNIT 2** Astronomy • **Lesson 6** *Stars/Sun/Secrets*

Classifying and Categorizing

### Practice and Apply

On the diagram below, heavenly bodies are categorized as stars, planets, and constellations. Complete the diagram by thinking of things that could be classified under the headings *Stars*, *Planets*, or *Constellations*.

HEAVENLY BODIES

Stars

Planets

Constellations

COMPREHENSION

# Quotation Marks, Underlining, and Apostrophes

| **Rule** | **Example** |
|---|---|
| ▶ A person's exact words are called a direct quotation. Enclose a direct quotation in quotation marks. | ▶ "You should get a flu shot," said the doctor. |
| ▶ Quotation marks are also used for the titles of poems, songs, and short stories. | ▶ I wrote a short story entitled "Maddie and the Bunny." |
| ▶ Underline titles of magazines, books, and long poems. | ▶ <u>*The Secret Garden*</u> |
| ▶ Apostrophes are used to show possession in most singular nouns and in contractions to indicate missing letters. | ▶ Tom's book is heavy. She'll (she will) try out for the team. |

**Insert quotation marks, apostrophes, and underlining to these sentences where needed.**

1. Benjamin Franklin said, Early to bed and early to rise makes a man healthy, wealthy, and wise.

2. The book, A Witness Tree, by Robert Frost, won a Pulitzer Prize for poetry.

3. We are reading the short story The Star in English class.

4. Did they say theyre on their way?

5. Id like to read the poem Turtle Island.

**UNIT 2** Back Through the Stars • **Lesson 6** *Stars*

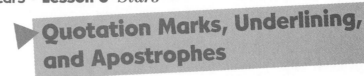

▶**Quotation Marks, Underlining, and Apostrophes**

## Practice

**Rewrite each title or contraction with the correct punctuation or underlining.**

**6.** My copy of the book The Rising Sun is at home.

_____

**7.** Who wrote the poem The Simple Truth?

_____

**8.** I'm looking for a book called Lincoln at Gettysburg.

_____

**9.** Theyd all like to join us. _____

**10.** Well be leaving tomorrow morning. _____

**11.** Youre all invited. _____

## Proofread

**Correct or add quotation marks and apostrophes in the paragraph below.**

Phoebe and I were discussing poetry. What poems did you last read? she asked.

I said, "Id have to check the title. I cant remember the whole name.

Phoebe asked, (What,s you're favorite poem of all time?)

I told her that its definitely I Can Dream.

Phoebe said, Id love to borrow it sometime."

**MECHANICS**

# Exact Words

| Rule | Example |
|---|---|
| ▶ Replace general nouns with specific ones. | ▶ *Before:* They cleared the trash from the park.<br>*Improved:* They cleared the park of its empty wrappers, discarded bottles, and fast-food containers. |
| ▶ Use colorful adjectives and avoid overused ones *(nice, fun, big,* and *great).* | ▶ *Before:* We had a great ride taking the cable car up the big mountain.<br>*Improved:* We had a thrilling ride taking the cable car up the towering mountain. |
| ▶ Choose precise, active verbs. | ▶ *Before:* She moved her hands away, but the card house fell.<br>*Improved:* She gently eased her hands away, but the card house tumbled. |

 **List at least three exact words that could be used to replace the overused word in each sentence.**

**1.** It was a *fun* game.

_____

**2.** You must *take* the trapeze when it swings back to you.

_____

**3.** The *small* chair is meant to be a toy.

_____

**4.** They *looked* out the window all day.

_____

**UNIT 2** Back Through the Stars • **Lesson 6** *Stars*

## Practice

**Rewrite each sentence. Replace the overused words with lively words having exact meanings. You may change other parts of the sentence as well, as long as the meaning is close to that of the original sentence.**

**5.** We thought the crystals in the museum exhibit were **pretty** and **interesting.**

_____

_____

**6.** The greenhouse air is **hot,** but the air outdoors is **cold.**

_____

_____

**7.** The thunder made a **loud noise.**

_____

**8.** My partner is **funny.**

_____

**9.** The cake was so **big** it wouldn't fit on the counter.

_____

**Rewrite this paragraph using exact words.**

**10.** We walked down the path toward the loud noise. When we came to the stream, we walked across it. The noise was louder when we came to a curve. We saw on our left a large section of woods being cut down. We saw a sign and walked over to it. We saw writing on the sign that said the site was to be the home of a new nature center.

_____

_____

WRITER'S CRAFT

**UNIT 2**   Back Through the Stars • **Lesson 7**   *The Book That Saved the Earth*

# Review

## Capitalization

**Draw three lines under letters that should be capitalized.**

1. Did you get tricked on april fools' day?

2. We visited yellowstone national park in wyoming.

3. Have you met senator hudson?

4. The colorado river flows through several states.

**Capitalize each proper noun.**

5. I prefer russian dressing rather than italian dressing.

_____

6. Where are the next olympics being held? _____

7. Do you know when *gone with the wind* was written?

_____

8. My spanish class is right before lunch. _____

**Draw three lines under letters that should be capital letters. Insert or cross out periods where needed.**

Dear Lindsay,

    Let's go to the library today and finish our research on the u s a. Our report is due on nov 4. I can meet today at 4:00 p.m.. Can mr Scott meet us there? I have an English test the same day and have some questions.

Your friend,<br>Kathy

ps I can also meet wed. night or sat. morning.

## ►Punctuation

**Rewrite the heading and inside address, adding commas where needed.**

Petaluma CA 96543 _____

July 2 2001 _____

Dr. Martha Barnett _____

52 Central Avenue _____

Newport Connecticut  22234 _____

**Insert hyphens, parentheses, and dashes where needed in the following paragraph.**

   Great philosophers thinkers developed the scientific method the principle of observation and experiment that is still the basis of scientific research today. Scientists start with observations and then make a hypothesis a guess. They must prove their hypothesis with trials and tests. For instance, seventeenth century scientist Isaac Newton used the scientific method when experimenting with sunlight passing through a prism.

**Rewrite each title or contraction with the correct punctuation or underlining.**

**9.** A Wrinkle in Time is one of my favorite books.

_____

**10.** We are reading the poem The Wind at the Door in English

class today. _____

**11.** Cecil wont be here today. _____

**12.** Shes going on a field trip. _____

MECHANICS

# Plot

> **Rule**
> ▶ A plot has a beginning, middle, and an end.
> ▶ The beginning section introduces the **problem.**
> ▶ In the middle section, characters experience conflict as they try to solve the problem or have things happen to them on the way to resolution.
> ▶ The **climax** or high point of action occurs when the problem is about to be solved, usually in the first part of the end section.
> ▶ The **conclusion,** also called the resolution, occurs after the climax and shows or tells how the problem is solved.

 **Try It!**  **Identify which part of a plot each situation describes. Write *problem, conflict, climax,* or *conclusion* for each description.**

1. We were about to give up hope when we saw a helicopter

   flying over the mountain toward us. _____

2. Tony and Kira were experienced climbers. Sonya and Ben were not. We knew that a town lay on the other side of the mountain, but we weren't sure if all four of us could

   climb the sharp peaks near the top. _____

3. The helicopter pilot rescued all four of us and radioed our

   families to let them know we were safe. _____

4. We had scaled three quarters of the mountain when Ben twisted his ankle. After taking turns supporting him on each side and moving upward slowly, we had to rest. Evening began to fall as we tried to think of a plan.

   _____

▶ **Plot**

**Practice**

**Write *problem* or *conclusion* to identify each of the following.**

**5.** To his relief, the lost luggage—including the suitcase with the important letters—arrived on his doorstep Sunday

morning. _____

**6.** A writer learns that the story idea she has been working

on has already been used by another writer. _____

**7.** The farm that the community was fighting to preserve will

not be turned into a golf course after all. _____

**Briefly describe a problem, conflict, climax, and conclusion to go with these story ideas.**

**8.** A group of dolphins is stranded on a beach.

Problem: _____

Conflict: _____

Climax: _____

Conclusion:_____

**9.** A weekend trip that a boy named Akeem takes to visit his grandmother turns out much differently than either of them expected.

Problem: _____

Conflict: _____

Climax: _____

Conclusion:_____

**WRITER'S CRAFT**

**UNIT 3** Heritage • **Lesson I** *The Land I Lost: Adventures of a Boy in Vietnam*

# Author's Purpose

**Focus** Authors always have a **purpose** in mind when they write a selection.

> An **author's purpose,** or reason for writing a selection, can be
> ▶ to inform, or give general information on a topic.
> ▶ to explain, or tell how something works or why something occurs.
> ▶ to persuade, or convince.
> ▶ to entertain, or interest and amuse.

## Identify

Look through "The Land I Lost: Adventures of a Boy in Vietnam" and complete the following. What was the author's purpose for writing this story? Give examples from the story that support your opinion.

Author' Purpose: _____

_____

Page: _____ Paragraph: _____

Example: _____

_____

_____

Page: _____ Paragraph: _____

Example: _____

_____

_____

**UNIT 3**  Heritage • **Lesson I**  *The Land I Lost: Adventures of a Boy in Vietnam*

▶ **Author's Purpose**

**Practice**

Read the paragraphs below and write the author's purpose for each one.

To grow tomatoes, first plant seeds in soil in small starter pots. Water the pots and set them in a sunny place. Within a few days, you should see the seedlings coming up. Be sure to keep the soil moist. When the seedlings are about a foot high, plant them outside. Water them immediately.

Author's Purpose: _____

Don't miss this year's community festival at Forest Park! The whole day promises to be fun filled. There will be games and activities for the entire family to enjoy. Free ice cream will be served between 4:00 and 6:00 P.M. Then, in the evening there will be live music and a special appearance by a surprise guest. Come be a part of all the fun!

Author's Purpose: _____

**Apply**

Write a paragraph about a person in history. Decide whether this paragraph will inform, explain, persuade, or entertain. Write its purpose. Then, write the paragraph.

_____

_____

_____

_____

_____

_____

**COMPREHENSION**

# Adjectives

| Rule | Example |
|---|---|
| ▶ Adjectives show what kind, how many, and which one. | ▶ We are studying **Egyptian** history. I have to read **three** chapters tonight. Our test is **this** Friday. |
| ▶ The words *a* and *an* are adjectives called indefinite articles. They can refer to any person, place, thing, or idea. Use *a* before a consonant sound and *an* before a vowel sound. | ▶ I took **a** photo of **an** ancient temple. |
| ▶ The word *the* is an adjective called a definite article. It refers to a specific person, place, thing, or idea. | ▶ We followed our tour guide through **the** pyramid. |
| ▶ Proper adjectives are formed from proper nouns. | ▶ A **British** scientist discovered King Tut's tomb in 1922. |
| ▶ Adjectives can be created by combining words with a hyphen. | ▶ We explored a **3,000-year-old** temple. |

**Circle the adjectives in this paragraph.**

An avalanche is a sudden, downward movement of snow and ice. An avalanche can send snow hurtling downhill at speeds of 160 kilometers an hour. In areas where avalanches are common, people sometimes create a controlled avalanche by setting explosives so they can control the slide.

**UNIT 3** Heritage • **Lesson I** *The Land I Lost*

▶ **Adjectives**

**GRAMMAR AND USAGE**

### Practice

**Write whether the bold word is an adjective that describes, points out, numbers, or is a definite or indefinite article. Indicate if the word is a proper adjective.**

1. **This** phone is broken. _____

2. That **French** architect is famous. _____

3. The recipe calls for **ten** apples. _____

4. **The** cabinet was fixed yesterday. _____

5. **These** monkeys are from Africa. _____

6. **Siamese** cats originated in Thailand. _____

7. Do you have **a** textbook? _____

### Proofread

**Cross out each adjective that is not used correctly and write above it the proper form of the adjective.**

It is possible an first celebration of Columbus' discovery

of America took place in New York City in 1792. These event

marked the 300st anniversary of his landing. President

Franklin D. Roosevelt made Columbus Day an legal holiday

in 1934.

On Columbus Day, we are reminded of an man who sailed

toward a unknown. His achievements encouraged an other

explorers to come to an Americas.

**UNIT 3**  Heritage • **Lesson 1** *The Land I Lost*

# Organization of a Descriptive Paragraph

**Rule**

▶ Descriptions may be organized from *top to bottom* or from *left to right.*

▶ Descriptions may organize from *front to back* or from *back to front.*

▶ Descriptions may be organized from *far to near* or from *near to far,* depending on what is described.

▶ Descriptions that organize by time may go from *most to least recent* or from *least to most recent.*

**Underline the main idea sentence. Double-underline the supporting sentences that contain descriptive details. Then write how each descriptive paragraph is organized.**

1. The weather has been crazy lately. Two days ago the sun was shining and it was 65 degrees outside. Yesterday we had freezing rain and then snow. Today it's raining, but tomorrow the forecast is for sun again with temperatures in the 60s.

   _____

2. This is what we see in the park. The pavilion stands at the far end from where we are standing. In front of the pavilion is the playground, and closer to where we are standing lies a large sandpit. We are standing in front of a sign that has a map and gives the history of the park.

   _____

**UNIT 3** Heritage • **Lesson I** *The Land I Lost*

## Organization of a Descriptive Paragraph

**Practice**

**3.** Draw a line to match each descriptive paragraph idea with the best way to organize the paragraph.

**Paragraph Ideas**

An orange,
beginning with the peel

The side of a long train

A pyramid

Things that happened
today, beginning with
what you just did

**Type of Organization**

top to bottom

outside to inside

most to least recent

left to right

**Write a descriptive paragraph for each of these ideas. Tell how you structured it.**

**4.** Describe a particular tree.

_____

_____

_____

Organized from _____ to _____

**5.** Describe what you might see looking outside a window in your home.

_____

_____

_____

Organized from _____ to _____

**WRITER'S CRAFT**

# Compare and Contrast

**Focus** Writers **compare** and **contrast** to paint a clearer picture of the people and things they are writing about.

> ▶ To **compare** means to tell how things, ideas, events, or characters are alike.
>
> ▶ To **contrast** means to tell how things, events, or characters are different.

## Identify

Look through "In Two Worlds: A Yup'ik Eskimo Family" and find contrasts between the Scammon Bay of Mary Anne's childhood and the Scammon Bay of today. What things have changed?

**1.** In Mary Anne's time: _____

_____

_____

Today: _____

_____

_____

**2.** In Mary Anne's time: _____

_____

_____

Today: _____

_____

▶**Compare and Contrast**

## Practice

Read each sentence and tell whether it shows a comparison or a contrast. Then, rewrite each sentence the other way. Note the change that occurs in the meaning.

1. Dave and Ed both finished all their vegetables. _____

_____

2. Martha plays the trombone, while Janet plays the cello. _____

_____

3. I like to read mysteries just like my sister Gina. _____

_____

4. Both cats and dogs make good pets. _____

_____

5. Jacob and Jason are twins, but Jacob is slightly taller. _____

_____

## Apply

Write a paragraph comparing and contrasting yourself to a friend or relative. Be sure to include ways that you are similar and ways that you are different.

_____

_____

_____

_____

COMPREHENSION

# Adverbs

| **Rule** | **Example** |
|---|---|
| ▶ An adverb modifies a verb, an adjective, or another adverb. Adverbs tell how or in what manner an action is done. | ▶ Our team played **wonderfully.** |
| ▶ Adverbs tell when an action is done. | ▶ Sarah was sick **today.** |
| ▶ Adverbs tell where an action is done. | ▶ Misha is waiting **here** for you. |
| ▶ Adverbs tell to what extent an action is done. | ▶ The captain is **always** on time. |

**Circle the adverbs in this paragraph.**

Scientists are working constantly to understand diseases. A disease can be relatively harmless or it may be quite serious. There are thousands of diseases that can strike almost any part of the body. Some diseases are chronic, such as arthritis, which makes the joints swell painfully. Other diseases are caused by harmful bacteria that invade the body. Poor living conditions can also cause disease.

**UNIT 3** Heritage • **Lesson 2** *In Two Worlds*

▶ **Adverbs**

**Practice**

| usually | often | also | about | typically | sometimes |

**Complete each sentence with an adverb from the words in the box that best fits in the sentence.**

The great white shark, _____ known as the white pointer, is considered to be more dangerous to humans than any other shark. It _____ lives in the open sea, but it _____ enters waters close to the shore. The white shark is known for its _____ dangerous attacks on small boats. The shark _____ grows to be _____ thirty-six feet long.

**Proofread**

**Add an adverb to each sentence to make the meaning clearer.**

Early settlers in the United States moved west in wagon trains. The settlers started in the morning around 4 A.M. They moved over mountains and through rivers. The settlers were glad for warm, dry weather. When the trail was muddy, the wagons were difficult to move. Oxen pulled the heavy wagons.

GRAMMAR AND USAGE

Name _____ Date _____

# Transition Words

Transition words structure descriptions having to do with time, place, and order. They also signal readers to expect comparisons, contrasts, additional information, and summaries. Some form two or more word phrases.

### Rule

▶ Transition words show time: *yesterday, the day before yesterday, this morning, today, tomorrow, tonight, this afternoon, this moment.*

▶ Transition words show order of occurrence: *earlier, about, as soon as, soon, finally, when, meanwhile, until, later, next, now, then, finally, last.*

▶ Transition words show contrast: *although, but, even, though, however, on the other hand, otherwise, still, while, yet, in contrast.*

▶ Use transition words to compare two things: *also, too, both, in the same way, just as, likewise, like, similarly.*

▶ Transition words signal additional information: *additionally, again, along with, also, and, another, besides, finally, for example, further, moreover.*

▶ Transition words introduce a conclusion or a summary: *as a result, finally, in conclusion, in summary, last, lastly, therefore.*

 **Transition words may be used for more than one purpose in a paragraph. Circle the transition words used below.**

1. Both Tiana and Maya like swimming, but Maya likes to swim freestyle and Tiana prefers the butterfly stroke. Both also swim the backstroke. Yesterday they practiced all three strokes for the meet today. This morning they woke up early, had a good breakfast, and did stretching exercises. This afternoon they will each swim in two events.

**UNIT 3** Heritage • **Lesson 2** *In Two Worlds*

**▶Transition Words**

**Practice**

**2.** Cross out the two transition words *least* likely to be used for each writing assignment.

| Writing Assignment | Transition Words |
|---|---|
| The end of a persuasive report | *in conclusion, yesterday, therefore, finally, underneath* |
| A description of a waterfall | *in summary, above, at the bottom, moreover, under* |
| A contrast of two books | *both, but, however, likewise, on the other hand* |

**3.** Use transition words that show location to describe a school bus.

_____

_____

**4.** Use transition words that signal additional information to describe a school policy.

_____

_____

**5.** Use transition words that compare and contrast to describe two different pets.

_____

_____

**6.** Use transition words to introduce the concluding paragraph for either an imaginary school report or for one you wrote earlier this year.

_____

**WRITER'S CRAFT**

# Prepositions

| Rule | Example |
|---|---|
| ▶ A preposition shows the relationship between a noun or a pronoun and another word in a sentence. | ▶ We walked **through** the blinding snowstorm. |
| ▶ The noun or pronoun that follows the preposition is the object of the preposition. | ▶ The dog slept under the **porch.** |
| ▶ A prepositional phrase is a group of words that begins with a preposition and ends with the object of the preposition. | ▶ The family took a trip **to the beach.** |

 **Try It!**  **Circle the prepositional phrases in this paragraph.**

Individual Chinese kingdoms began building what would become the Great Wall around the seventh century B.C. The wall was started in the northern part of the kingdom's capital. Other states started building walls for protection during the sixth century. In the third century B.C., the first emperor of China connected the walls into one system. The Great Wall extends 4,160 miles across China's countryside. Many tourists today still visit what remains of the wall.

**UNIT 3** Heritage • **Lesson 3** *The West Side*

▶ **Prepositions**

**GRAMMAR AND USAGE**

### Practice

**Write sentences using these prepositions in a prepositional phrase.**

**1.** after _____

**2.** at _____

**3.** from _____

**4.** on _____

**5.** under _____

**6.** with _____

### Proofread

**Improve the paragraph below by adding at least four prepositional phrases to give more information.**

Jonah likes to skateboard. He often goes with his brother. They prefer the lot next to the big oak trees. Many kids come here to skate. There is a lot of competition. However, they also enjoy teaching each other new tricks they learned. Their parents sometimes sit and watch them skate.

**UNIT 3** Heritage • **Lesson 3** *The West Side*

# Sensory Details

Sensory detail re-creates the look, sound, feel, smell, and/or taste of whatever is described. Sensory description uses details that rely on one or more of the major senses.

| **Rule** | **Example** |
|---|---|
| ▶ It recalls **sight** to create detailed visual pictures. | ▶ Before the storm, the sky turned shades of green, dark blue, and gray. |
| ▶ It recalls **sound** to engage the reader's sense of hearing. | ▶ We heard thunder muttering in the distance. |
| ▶ It recalls **touch** to re-create how something feels. | ▶ Large, warm drops of rain fell on our arms and faces. |
| ▶ It recalls **smell** to create a mental image of how something smells. | ▶ We stepped in the house and smelled the sweet aroma of apple pie. |
| ▶ It recalls **taste** to appeal to the reader's sense of taste. | ▶ The sweet, tangy taste of the apple pie was the high point of the evening. |

 **Draw a line to match the sensory description to its related sense.**

The go-cart steering wheel was softly padded.                 sight

Gas fumes greeted us at the track.                 taste

Loud, uneven rumbling filled the air.                 smell

The course formed a large figure eight.                 touch

The mouth-watering pizza we ate                 sound
hit the spot.

**UNIT 3** Heritage • **Lesson 3** *The West Side*

▶ **Sensory Details**

**WRITER'S CRAFT**

( **Practice** )

**Descriptive paragraphs often provide readers with more than one sensory detail. List the sensory details and the related senses used in this paragraph.**

1. The Ferris wheel towered over the fairground. From the parking lot we could hear the droning of the rides and the excited screams of riders. As we walked closer, an aroma of peanuts filled the air, and we couldn't resist buying some. We cracked the brittle shells and devoured the salty, crunchy nuts.

_____

_____

_____

_____

_____

**Go to or imagine being in a place rich in sensation, such as your desk, the library, or the playground. Write descriptions that include sensory details appealing to each of the five major senses. Use your imagination for senses that cannot be used at the present moment.**

2. Sight _____

3. Hearing _____

4. Touch _____

5. Smell _____

6. Taste _____

Name _____ Date _____

# Making Inferences

**Focus** Good readers can **make inferences** about a character or event in a story.

> **Making inferences** is using information from the text, along with one's own experiences or knowledge, to
> ▶ get a fuller understanding of story characters.
> ▶ figure out a more complete picture of story events.

## Identify

Make an inference about the following characters from "Love As Strong As Ginger." Then, write down the examples from the story that helped you make the inference.

**Gnin Gnin:** _____

_____

_____

**Examples:** _____

_____

_____

**Katie:** _____

_____

_____

**Examples:** _____

_____

_____

**UNIT 3** Heritage • **Lesson 4** *Love As Strong As Ginger*

**Making Inferences**

### Practice

Prepare to write a paragraph that will leave out information for the reader to infer. First, choose a famous person and write down his or her name. Then, list some characteristics or other information about the person.

Famous person: _____

Characteristics or other information: _____

_____

_____

_____

### Apply

Now, use your notes to write a paragraph about the person you chose. Do not use the person's name in your paragraph. Cover the section above and show your paragraph to a classmate to see if he or she can infer from your paragraph who the person is.

_____

_____

_____

_____

_____

_____

_____

_____

COMPREHENSION

**UNIT 3**  Heritage • **Lesson 4**  *Love as Strong as Ginger*

# Conjunctions and Interjections

| **Rule** | **Example** |
|---|---|
| ▶ A coordinating conjunction joins words or groups of words that are equally important in a sentence. Some coordinating conjunctions include *and, but, or, so, nor, yet,* and *for*. | ▶ Barbara **and** Angela are on the soccer team. |
| ▶ A correlative conjunction connects compound parts of a sentence. It includes *both . . . and, either . . . or,* and *not only . . . but also*. | ▶ We are going **either** to the museum or to the library. |
| ▶ Subordinating conjunctions connect two clauses where one clause is dependent on the other. Some subordinating conjunctions include *after, although, before, if, when,* and *while*. | ▶ Raise your hand **when** I call your name. |
| ▶ An interjection expresses strong feeling. | ▶ **Wow!** The Empire State Building is 1,250 feet high! |

 **Try It!**  **Fill in each blank with an interjection or conjunction from the words in the box.**

| while | but | because | wow |
|---|---|---|---|

1. _____! What a pitch!

2. _____ the cake is cooling, I'll make the frosting.

3. It is cloudy, _____ it doesn't look stormy.

4. Yolanda couldn't go _____ she was sick.

**UNIT 3**  Heritage • **Lesson 4**  *Love as Strong as Ginger*

## Conjunctions and Interjections

### Practice

**Write two sentences using conjunctions.**

1. _____

2. _____

**Write two sentences using interjections.**

3. _____

4. _____

### Proofread

**Add conjunctions to the paragraph below.**

Thomas Jefferson wrote the Declaration of Independence. On July 4, 1776, the leaders of the colonies all agreed to adopt it. Most Americans were happy about it. The real celebration could not take place yet. People from every colony went to war against England. Many battles were fought. Many lives were lost. Ben Franklin worked to help his city, Philadelphia. He also worked to help all the colonies. July 4, 1776, is still important to us today. It is the birthday of our country.

GRAMMAR AND USAGE

**UNIT 3**  Heritage • **Lesson 4** *Love as Strong as Ginger*

# Sound of Language

The sound of language refers to the sounds that words make. Pay attention to how words create sounds and effects so you can craft your own writing to appeal to your reader's sense of sound.

| **Rule** | **Example** |
|---|---|
| ▶ When you use **alliteration,** you repeat the consonant sounds that begin words. | ▶ The **w**ind **wh**ispered **wh**en it blew through the **w**illow trees. |
| ▶ When you use **assonance,** you repeat vowel sounds, usually within words. | ▶ There was nothing t**o** d**o** but gaze at the s**oo**thing bl**ue** sea. |
| ▶ When you use **onomatopoeia,** you use a word(s) that imitates the sound made by or associated with the thing that you are describing. | ▶ The **clashing** and **clanging** pans in the kitchen startled us. |
| ▶ **End rhyme** (often used in poetry) refers to rhyming words at the end of lines. | ▶ He washed and dressed and then he **ate;** We, unfortunately, were very **late.** |
| ▶ **Internal rhyme** refers to rhyme that occurs in the middle of lines. | ▶ Please shut the d**oor** be**fore** you leave. |

 **Try It!**  **Draw a line to match each group of words with the sound technique used.**

baa, sizzle, whack, meow                    assonance

rat, bath, pack, last                       alliteration

run, rain, ripe, royal                      rhyme

frame, game, tame, same                     onomatopoeia

Name _____ Date _____

▶ **Sound of Language**

**Practice**

**Write *alliteration, assonance, onomatopoeia, end rhyme,* or *internal rhyme* to show how these sentences play with the sound of language.**

**1.** Get into great shape by playing your favorite outdoor

game. _____

**2.** I like to hike with Mike and Jamal. _____

**3.** What is that buzzing sound? _____

**4.** We never thought we'd find a space;
As each car left, a new one took its place.

_____

**5.** I'm going to zip over to Zach's house so we can do our

zebra report. _____

**Write sentences using the specified technique.**

**6.** Write a sentence using alliteration. Use the beginning
sounds *s, ch,* or *b.*

_____

**7.** Write a sentence using assonance. Use words with the
long *i* sound as in *pie.*

_____

**8.** Write a sentence using onomatopoeia. Use one or more of
these onomatopoeic words: *giggle, sniffle, rattle, squish.*

_____

WRITER'S CRAFT

# Pronouns

| Rule | Example |
| --- | --- |
| ▶ A possessive pronoun shows ownership. It can be used alone or before a noun. | ▶ The book is **his.** This is **my** brother. |
| ▶ A reflexive pronoun ends with *-self* or *-selves* and refers to the subject. | ▶ I made **myself** a sandwich. |
| ▶ An intensive pronoun ends with *-self* or *-selves* and emphasizes a noun or pronoun. | ▶ Angela **herself** will design the float. |
| ▶ An indefinite pronoun does not refer to a specific person, place, thing, or idea. | ▶ **Anyone** can attend the study session. |

## Try It!

**Circle the pronouns in this paragraph.**

   Belinda and I are good friends. We wanted to visit the museum together. Our parents said that they would take us. My mom dropped Belinda and me off at the front door of the museum. We had four hours before Belinda's dad was going to pick us up. We were so excited to be able to go by ourselves. I wore my backpack, and Belinda wore hers. She wanted to get her brother a poster at the museum for his room. We love the museum and its special exhibits.

**Pronouns**

## Practice

**Circle the correct pronoun.**

My friend Suzanne and  **I  me**  think voting should be required.  **Us  We**  believe that people owe it to **theirselves  themselves**  and society to vote. Of course, some people think that required voting would interfere with **their  them**  freedom of choice. Most people, however, agree on  **it's  its**  importance.

## Proofread

**Cross out the incorrect pronoun forms and write the correct form above it.**

Bennett called Sandra and I last week. Him and several

others were planning to visit several spots along the Oregon

Trail. Him told we it was about 2,000 miles long. It's starting

point was at Independence, Missouri, the westernmost

settlement in the days of the pioneers. Bennett has hisself

walked several miles on the trail.

**GRAMMAR AND USAGE**

# Figurative Language

These types of figurative language are used in writing:

| **Rule** | **Example** |
|---|---|
| ▶ A **simile** compares two unlike things by using either *like* or *as*. | ▶ He carried the computer parts as if they were eggs. |
| ▶ A **metaphor** compares two unlike things without using *like* or *as*. | ▶ Our backyard was a lake after the six days of rain. |
| ▶ **Personification** gives nonhuman things or ideas qualities that are human. | ▶ The moon's bright face smiled down at us when we went for a late night swim. |
| ▶ **Hyperbole** is extreme exaggeration. Often used for humorous effect, it may describe a quality of one thing by comparing it to that of another. | ▶ After six days of rain, we had a puddle the size of the Atlantic Ocean in our back yard. |
| ▶ An **idiom** is a phrase that cannot be understood by knowing only the literal meaning. It is an expression that is unique to a certain language. | ▶ When our dog Buddy is groomed, he feels like a million dollars. |

 **Write the figure of speech—*simile, metaphor, personification, hyperbole,* or *idiom*—used in each sentence.**

1. The tree stump dug in its heels and stubbornly refused to

   budge. _____

2. You've done so much work; you can call it a day. _____

3. Our cat dashes like a streak of lightning when she sees

   the delivery truck. _____

4. I wore out my shoes looking for you. _____

5. The line to the gym was a snake. _____

**UNIT 3** Heritage • **Lesson 5** *The Night Journey*

▶ **Figurative Language**

**Practice**

**Write a sentence for each figure of speech listed. Use an idea provided or one of your own.**

6. Write a simile. Ideas: how you feel at the end of the day; how you or someone else writes.

_____

_____

7. Write a metaphor. Ideas: what your room looks like before you clean it; what your room looks like after you clean it.

_____

_____

8. Write a sentence using personification. Ideas: a mountain; a bumpy road.

_____

_____

9. Write a sentence using hyperbole. Ideas: a time you had to hurry; a time you ate too much.

_____

_____

10. Write a sentence using one of these idioms: something up your sleeve; hit the hay.

_____

_____

**WRITER'S CRAFT**

# ▶Review

## ▶Adjectives

**Write three adjectives that could be used to describe each of these nouns.**

1. skateboard _____ _____ _____

2. parade _____ _____ _____

3. family _____ _____ _____

4. game _____ _____ _____

5. joke _____ _____ _____

## ▶Adverbs

**Circle the adverbs in this paragraph.**

   Although people often say that bread is the staff of life, few people know much about bread, except that it is easily purchased in the grocery store. Nobody knows exactly when the first grass seeds were ground and baked into bread, but remains of the Swiss Lake Dwellers positively prove that man already was baking bread in prehistoric times.

## ▶Prepositions

**Write a sentence using these prepositions in a prepositional phrase.**

6. above _____

7. during _____

8. into _____

9. of _____

▶ **Conjunctions and Interjections**

**Write two sentences using conjunctions.**

10. _____

11. _____

**Write two sentences using interjections.**

12. _____

13. _____

▶ **Pronouns**

**Circle the correct pronoun in these sentences.**

14. Anna and **he   him**   plan to buy the boat.

15. **Us   We**   soccer players got new uniforms.

16. When are you and **he   him**   coming to see me?

17. The team and **us   we**   have to leave.

18. **He   Him**   and **her   she**   got married.

19. Our school is the first of **it's   its**   kind.

20. He helped **himself   hisself**   to more salad.

21. They got **theirselves   themselves**   into trouble.

**Write two sentences using indefinite pronouns.**

22. _____

23. _____

# Exact Words

Use exact words in your writing to help readers better imagine what it is you are describing. Replace words that are overused or too general with words that are precise and lively.

### Rule

▸ Replace general nouns with specific ones.

▸ Use colorful adjectives and avoid overused ones such as *nice*, *great*, and *fun*.

▸ Choose precise, active verbs.

### Example

▸ *Before:* He likes some of their things.
*Improved:* He likes their frozen yogurt, tacos, and fruit salad.

▸ *Before:* That was a fun ride.
*Improved:* That was a thrilling ride.

▸ *Before:* Samantha took two of each kind.
*Improved:* Samantha carefully chose two of each kind.

 **Try It!** **List at least three exact words that could be used to replace the overused word(s) in each sentence.**

1. It was a **very nice** live butterfly exhibit.

_____

2. **Put** that piece there and **put** the smaller piece inside the square.

_____

3. There was a **great big** package outside the door.

_____

4. We **walked** carefully toward the noise.

_____

**UNIT 3** Heritage • **Lesson 6** *Parmele*

### Practice

**Rewrite each sentence. Replace the overused words with lively words having exact meanings. You may change other parts of the sentence as well, as long as the meaning is close to that of the original sentence.**

5. I looked inside the package.

_____

6. The salamanders moved quickly in all directions.

_____

7. The quietness surprised us.

_____

8. It was an interesting story.

_____

9. Paul is a good cook.

_____

**Rewrite this paragraph using exact words.**

10. It was a pretty place to be. The lake was very pretty and beyond that were the mountains, which were also very nice. Lots of pretty wildflowers were growing around the lake. We were happy to spend the day there.

_____

_____

_____

_____

**WRITER'S CRAFT**

**Exact Words**

# Cause and Effect

**Focus**  Writers often provide clues that signal cause-and-effect relationships for the events described in their writing.

When one event causes another to happen, the events have a **cause-and-effect relationship**.
► A cause is an event that makes it possible for another event to happen.
► An effect is the result of an event.
► Words such as *because, since, therefore,* and *so* are clues to the reader that a cause-and-effect relationship has taken place.

## Identify

Skim the selection ". . . If You Lived at the Time of the American Revolution" to find out why the following events happened. Write down the cause for each event.

**1.** The Patriots dumped England's tea into Boston Harbor

because _____

**2.** The British soldiers were called "Redcoats" because

_____

**3.** Many families were split because _____

_____

**4.** Certain soldiers in the Continental Army were called

"minutemen" because _____

**5.** During the war, paper money lost value because

_____

**UNIT 4**  Making a New Nation • **Lesson 1**  *If You Lived at the Time of the American Revolution/Yankee Doodle*

▶ **Cause and Effect**

**COMPREHENSION**

## Practice

Some of the sentences below show causes, and other sentences show effects. Complete each sentence by adding the missing part of the cause-and-effect relationship.

**1.** Angelina was covered in mud, therefore _____

_____

**2.** The music teacher did not show up for class, so _____

_____

**3.** Kristi suddenly laughed out loud because _____

_____

**4.** Since it was raining outside, _____

_____

## Apply

Write a paragraph that includes at least three cause-and-effect relationships. You might use one of the sentences above to begin your paragraph.

_____

_____

_____

_____

_____

_____

# Types of Sentences

| **Rule** | **Example** |
|---|---|
| ▶ A **clause** is a group of words that has a subject and a verb. An **independent clause** can stand alone as a sentence. | ▶ The barn will be painted. |
| ▶ A **dependent clause** has a subject and a verb but cannot stand alone as a sentence. | ▶ **When the workers arrive,** the barn will be painted. |
| ▶ A **simple sentence** has one subject and one predicate. It may have a compound subject or predicate. | ▶ George Washington and John Adams were the first two presidents. |
| ▶ A **compound sentence** contains two or more simple sentences. | ▶ George Washington lived in Mount Vernon, and Thomas Jefferson lived at Monticello. |
| ▶ A **complex sentence** contains a dependent clause and an independent clause. | ▶ While George Washington was president, John Adams was vice president. |
| ▶ A **fragment** does not express a complete thought. | ▶ Signed the Declaration of Independence. |
| ▶ A **run-on sentence** is two or more sentences incorrectly written as though they are one. | ▶ We went to the zoo it was fun. |

 **Try It!** Write *simple, compound,* or *complex* to tell the type of sentence.

1. _____ Stalin, Roosevelt, and Churchill met at a conference at Yalta.

2. _____ They met before World War II ended.

3. _____ Everything was not resolved, but some big decisions were made.

**GRAMMAR AND USAGE**

▶ **Types of Sentences**

## Practice

**Tell whether each group of words is a sentence. Write *yes* or *no*.**

1. _____ Tropical zones lie north and south of the equator.

2. _____ Within one city, temperatures may vary dramatically during the year.

3. _____ Mount Kilimanjaro on a map.

4. _____ Has snow near its peak.

5. _____ Elevation also affects temperature air becomes less dense at higher altitudes.

6. _____ Most of Earth's people live in the temperate zones.

## Proofread

**Separate the sentences in the following paragraph by inserting the correct end punctuation. Draw three lines under letters that should be capitalized.**

have you ever had to write a paper before you start to

write, you must decide the purpose of your writing. Is it a

story or does it describe something or do you want to inform?

Maybe you want to persuade your readers about something

maybe you want to entertain your audience. Think about who

your audience is you may even want to write just for yourself.

What a great audience you are

# Aim/Purpose/Audience

Determine your aim, purpose, and audience before you write so you can better plan the information, ideas, and language you use.

| **Rule** | **Example** |
| --- | --- |
| ▶ Your **aim** is your specific goal, focus, or reason for writing. | ▶ You write an advertisement in your school newspaper announcing the school lip sync competition. The aim is to get students to participate. |
| ▶ Your **purpose** is more general. It is *why* you are writing— to inform, to explain, to entertain, or to persuade. | ▶ The purpose for an advertisement for a lip sync competition is to persuade. |
| ▶ Your **audience** refers to your readers. The information and language you use in your writing should appeal to your readers' interests, experience, and level of understanding. | ▶ For the lip sync advertisement, you use language that emphasizes fun and appeals to the students' interest in music. |

 **Try It!**   **Read each book title. Label the author's purpose by writing *inform*, *explain*, *entertain*, or *persuade* in the first blank. List a possible audience in the second space.**

**1.** A Tale of Two Turkeys _____

_____

**2.** How to Roast the Perfect Turkey _____

_____

**3.** The Real History of the first Thanksgiving _____

_____

**WRITER'S CRAFT**

▶ **Aim/Purpose/Audience**

**Practice**

Write what you think is the author's aim, purpose, and audience for the following.

4.

| **Handy Hardware** |
| **We Happen to Have It All!** |

Seeds
Bones, Rawhide
Bargains Bona-fide,
Come Inside!

Aim:

Purpose:

Audience:

5. A message at the bottom of the television screen that says "Severe thunderstorm expected to hit Chester, Montgomery, and Delaware counties around midnight tonight."

Aim:

Purpose:

Audience:

**UNIT 4**  Making a New Nation • **Lesson 2** *The Night the Revolution Began*

# Subject and Verb Agreement

| **Rule** | **Example** |
| --- | --- |
| ▶ The singular form of present tense verbs usually ends in *-s* or *-es*. | ▶ She **sits** at the table by the window. |
| ▶ The singular form of regular past tense verbs usually ends in *-d* or *-ed*. | ▶ June **rented** a movie to watch with her brother. |
| ▶ Irregular past tense verbs are formed in a way other than by adding *-d* or *-ed*. | ▶ Terri **went** with Tom to the skating rink. |
| ▶ A compound subject—two or more subjects connected by *and*—uses the plural form of the verb. | ▶ Carmen and Yasushi **eat** in the cafeteria. |

 **Try It!**

**Write the past tense of the following verbs. Check your dictionary if you need to.**

**1.** know _____

**2.** see _____

**3.** climb _____

**4.** run _____

**5.** swim _____

**6.** throw _____

**7.** become _____

**UNIT 4** Making a New Nation • **Lesson 2** *The Night the Revolution Began*

▶ **Subject and Verb Agreement**

## Practice

**Rewrite each pair of sentences as one sentence with a compound subject. Use the correct verb.**

**1.** Hiro got new in-line skates. Mai Lin got new in-line skates.

_____

**2.** Trent likes to play chess. Joy likes to play chess.

_____

**3.** Two bishops are needed to start a chess game. Two knights are needed to start a chess game.

_____

_____

## Proofread

**Correct the errors in subject-verb agreement in the following paragraph by crossing out the incorrect verb and writing the correct verb above it.**

Chess first appeared in India about the sixth century A.D.

Since the 15th century, chess have been known as the "royal

game" because of its popularity among kings and queens.

The board represent a battlefield in which two armies fights

to captured each other's king. A player's army consist of

16 pieces. Interest in chess explode during the twentieth

century. Players competes for tournament prizes. Organized

chess tournaments and Internet chess now attract people

around the world.

**UNIT 4** Making a New Nation • **Lesson 2** *The Night the Revolution Began*

# Transition Words

### Rule

▶ Transition words show **time:** *yesterday, this morning, this afternoon, today, this evening, tonight, this afternoon, at present, this moment*

▶ Transition words show **order of occurrence:** *earlier, about, as soon as, soon, finally, first, when, meanwhile, until, later, next, now, then, last*

▶ Transition words show **contrast:** *although, but, however, on the other hand,* or **comparison:** *also, just as, in the same way, similarly, likewise*

▶ Transition words signal **additional** or **more important** information: *additionally, again, also, and, another, besides, finally, more importantly*

▶ Transition words introduce a **conclusion** or the **points of a summary:** *as a result, finally, in conclusion, in summary, last, lastly, therefore*

▶ Transition words take readers through **place and location** descriptions: *on top, under, below, beneath, underneath, to the left, left, right, to the far right*

1. Circle only the transition words that would be useful for ending a report on the importance of space exploration.

   *on the bottom, in summary, lastly, in contrast, therefore, to the far right, this morning, in conclusion, finally*

2. Circle the transition words that would be most useful for a writing assignment on what and how you would pack for a long trip.

   *first, therefore, along with, in addition, next, then, in contrast, last, likewise, in summary, also*

**UNIT 4** Making a New Nation • **Lesson 2** *The Night the Revolution Began*

▶ **Transition Words**

**WRITER'S CRAFT**

**Practice**

**3.** Draw a line to match the writing topic to the transition
words.

| **Writing Topic** | **Transition Words** |
|---|---|
| A comparison/contrast of two different brands of the same type of cereal | yesterday, this afternoon, tomorrow, in two days |
| A day-by-day description of when someone exercises | first, next, then, last |
| Written instructions on giving a dog a bath | similarly, just as, also, both, in contrast, on the other hand |

**Choose two of the above writing topics for which to write
paragraphs. Use the matching transition words along with any
of your own. Be sure to include a main idea sentence stating
your topic. Circle the transition words.**

**4.** _____

_____

_____

_____

**5.** _____

_____

_____

_____

_____

**UNIT 4**  Making a New Nation • **Lesson 3**  *The Midnight Ride of Paul Revere*

# Misused Words

| Rule | Example |
|---|---|
| ▶ The verb *lie* means "to rest or recline." | ▶ I like to **lie** on the couch after a big meal. |
| ▶ The verb *lay* means "to place or put an object somewhere." | ▶ You shouldn't **lay** your coat on the floor. |
| ▶ The verb *sit* means "to rest or to have a seat." | ▶ I usually **sit** in the front row. |
| ▶ The verb *set* means "to put or place something." | ▶ Will you **set** that plate on the counter? |
| ▶ Use *may* to ask or give permission. Use *can* to show ability to do something. | ▶ **May** I use the phone? I **can** get that for you. |

**Try It!**

**Circle the correct word for each sentence.**

1. Rashad wants to  **lay   lie**   down.

2. Did you  **set   sit**   the vase where I asked you to?

3. The students  **raised   rose**   the flag this morning.

4. You  **can   may**   attend the play.

5. Did you like  **it's   its**   ending?

6. Tom liked it better  **than   then**   the movie.

7. I thought the play was  **to   too**   long.

**UNIT 4** Making a New Nation • **Lesson 3** *The Midnight Ride of Paul Revere*

**Misused Words**

**GRAMMAR AND USAGE**

## Practice

**Use a form of *sit-set* or *lie-lay* to complete each sentence.**

**1.** Where did you _____ that box?

**2.** After it had _____ for a while, the computer started up just fine.

**3.** I need to _____ down and rest.

**4.** Your books are _____ all over the room.

**5.** I am restless after _____ here all day.

## Proofread

**Cross out each incorrect word and write the correct word above it.**

Sound waves may travel in many different ways. You can't actually see sound waves, but their is an experiment you can do to prove they are real. First, punch a hole in the bottoms of to paper cups and then sit them upside down. Put a string through the first hole and the second one, to, and then tie a knot at each end. Take one cup, give the other to a friend, and then move far apart, making sure the string is tight. Rise one of the cups too your mouth and than talk. The person holding the cup on the other end will here your voice because the vibrations of the string carry the sound.

# Sentence Elaboration and Expansion

| **Rule** | **Example** |
|---|---|
| ▶ Short sentences may be changed into prepositional or participial phrases and attached to other sentences. | ▶ *Before:* My journal is safely hidden. It is in my top drawer. It is under my socks. *Improved:* My journal is safely hidden in my top drawer, under my socks. |
| ▶ Short sentences may be changed into adjective or adverb clauses and attached to other sentences. | ▶ *Before:* We don't have any homework. It's Friday. We are going to go bowling. *Improved:* Because we don't have any homework and it's Friday, we are going to go bowling. |
| ▶ Appositives and appositive phrases may be combined with independent clauses to cut down on the need for short, explanatory sentences. | ▶ *Before:* Mr. Fernandez is our teacher. He grew up in Argentina. *Improved:* Mr. Fernandez, our teacher, grew up in Argentina. |

 **Write whether each expanded sentence uses a prepositional phrase, an appositive, or an adverb clause.**

1. The blue whale, the largest animal in the world, can grow to be 100 feet long and may weigh up to 150 tons.

_____

2. The blue whale dove calmly into the depths as if she were the queen of the ocean.

_____

3. After straining the tiny creatures through its baleen, a blue whale may eat up to four tons of krill in just one day.

_____

**UNIT 4** Making a New Nation • **Lesson 3** *The Midnight Ride of Paul Revere*

**Practice**

**Change the following short sentences to expanded sentences by converting them to prepositional or participial phrases, adjective or adverb clauses, or appositives. Attach them to independent clauses.**

**4.** We went to the marine park. We wanted to go, because we had free passes. We wanted to see the Magellanic penguins.

_____

_____

_____

**5.** There were fish swimming under the bridge. There were fish swimming in and out of the coral. Fish swam everywhere.

_____

_____

**6.** We saw the penguins do different things. The penguins were shaking out their feathers. The penguins were swimming quickly through the water. The penguins were searching for fish.

_____

_____

_____

**7.** There is a group of researchers. They study king penguins. They tagged several. The penguins live on islands near Antarctica.

_____

_____

_____

WRITER'S CRAFT

# Classifying and Categorizing

**Focus** Readers classify and categorize ideas, events, people, and objects to help them remember or identify how they are related.

> To **classify** means to group ideas, events, people, and objects according to their similarities.
>
> A **category** is the actual group into which similar things are placed. Things can often fit into more than one category.

## Identify

Review the selection "The Declaration of Independence" for examples of text in which ideas, events, people, and things are classified and categorized. Write your examples on the lines.

Page: _____ Paragraph: _____

Example: _____

_____

_____

_____

_____

Page: _____ Paragraph: _____

Example: _____

_____

_____

_____

_____

**UNIT 4** Making a New Nation • **Lesson 4** *The Declaration of Independence*

**Classifying and Categorizing**

### Practice

Choose an aspect of the Declaration of Independence or the American Revolution in general to classify and categorize. Use the chart below to organize the information into categories. You can add columns if necessary.

| | | |
|---|---|---|
| | | |
| | | |

### Apply

In the space below, write a paragraph using the information you classified and categorized above. Include your classifications in your paragraph to help organize your thoughts.

_____

_____

_____

_____

_____

_____

_____

**COMPREHENSION**

**UNIT 4**  Making a New Nation • **Lesson 4**  *The Declaration of Independence*

# Comparative and Superlative Adjectives and Adverbs

| **Rule** | **Example** |
| --- | --- |
| ▶ A comparative adjective compares one person or thing with another. | ▶ It is **colder** outside today than it was yesterday. |
| ▶ A superlative adjective compares one person or thing with several others. | ▶ This is the **most interesting** bird I have ever seen. |
| ▶ Comparative adverbs compare two actions. | ▶ The tutor arrived **earlier** than her student did. |
| ▶ Superlative adverbs compare one action with several others. | ▶ Of all land animals, cheetahs run **most rapidly.** |

**Write the comparative and superlative forms of each adjective.**

**1.** late _____

**2.** low _____

**3.** bright _____

**4.** fearful _____

**5.** bad _____

**6.** good _____

**7.** pretty _____

**8.** famous _____

Name _____ Date _____

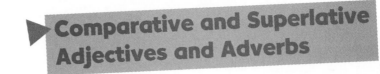

**GRAMMAR AND USAGE**

### Practice

**For each sentence, write the correct form of the adjective or adverb in parentheses.**

1. It used to be slightly _____ than São Paulo. (populous)

2. Of all centuries, the world population has grown

   _____ in the twentieth century. (rapid)

3. The bicycle is still the _____ form of personal transportation in China. (common)

4. Of all countries, Germany has the _____ record of all nations for recycling waste. (good)

### Proofread

**Cross out the incorrect form of each superlative adjective and adverb in the following paragraph and write the correct form above it.**

Animals are the interestingest and sometimes the

most strangest living things on Earth. Did you know that

the Goliath beetle, weighing 3.5 ounces, is the most heaviest

insect in the world? The sailfish, at 68 miles per hour,

swims quickliest of all fish. The Australian sea wasp has

the more painfulest sting of all animals. The two-toed sloth

moves slowest than any other mammal and spends most

of its life in trees. Howler monkeys yell louder of all primates.

Their voices can be heard up to three miles away.

**UNIT 4** Making a New Nation • **Lesson 4** *The Declaration of Independence*

# Passive Voice

When overused, the **passive voice,** in which the subject receives the action of the verb, leads to writing that is dull and lifeless. For lively, engaging writing, use the **active voice.** In the active voice, the subject performs the action of the verb.

| **Rule** | **Example** |
|---|---|
| ▶ Use the active voice unless you have a good reason to use the passive. | ▶ *Active:* My brother *served* breakfast. *Passive:* Breakfast *was served* by my brother. |
| ▶ The passive voice is a verb form made with a form of the helping verb *be* followed by a past participle. | ▶ The bicycle tire *was patched* by my grandmother. |
| ▶ Convert the passive voice to the active voice in some sentences by moving the *subject* of the sentence. | ▶ My *grandmother* patched the bicycle tire. |
| ▶ Do not shift to passive voice when a sentence begins with the active voice. | ▶ *Active:* When we came home, we saw a groundhog in our yard. *Shift to Passive:* When we came home, a groundhog was seen in our yard. |

 **Try It!** Underline the sentence in each pair that uses the active voice. Draw a line through the sentence that uses the passive voice.

1. The car was washed yesterday by my aunt.
   My aunt washed the car yesterday.

2. When we looked in the closet, we found the art materials.
   When we looked in the closet, the art materials were found.

3. The cake was baked yesterday by Cameron.
   Cameron baked the cake yesterday.

**UNIT 4**    Making a New Nation • **Lesson 4** *The Declaration of Independence*

▶ **Passive Voice**

**Practice**

These sentences use the passive voice. Write a new sentence for each example using the active voice.

4. The book was read by everybody in our class.

_____

5. All the good seats were taken by the fourth graders.

_____

6. The garden was weeded by our family on Saturday.

_____

7. The mural was painted by Ms. Liem's fifth-grade class.

_____

8. My homework was finished by five o'clock on Tuesday.

_____

9. When we walked out onto the balcony, pigeons were seen flying away.

_____

_____

10. Write a description of what you see on your way to school, using the active voice.

_____

_____

_____

_____

_____

**WRITER'S CRAFT**

# Drawing Conclusions

**Focus** Writers do not always provide complete descriptions or detailed information about a topic, character, thing, or event, so readers must draw their own conclusions.

> **Drawing Conclusions** requires readers to
> ▶ make statements about topics, events, characters, or things based on information from the text.

## Identify

Skim the selection "The Master Spy of Yorktown." Then, next to each person's name below, write a statement (draw a conclusion) about him. Then record the text clues on which you based your conclusions.

The Marquis de Lafayette: _____

Clues: _____

_____

_____

_____

James Armistead: _____

Clues: _____

_____

_____

_____

**UNIT 4** Making a New Nation • **Lesson 5** *The Master Spy of Yorktown*

▶ **Drawing Conclusions**

## Practice and Apply

Write about a character, topic, thing, or event. Before you begin writing, identify a specific conclusion about your subject that you want readers to draw. Write a paragraph about your subject below. Then exchange papers with a partner. When you have finished reading each other's papers, write a conclusion you have drawn and the text clues that support it at the bottom of the page.

_____

_____

_____

_____

_____

_____

_____

_____

_____

_____

_____

Conclusion: _____

_____

_____

_____

COMPREHENSION

# Direct and Indirect Objects

| **Rule** | **Example** |
|---|---|
| ▶ A **direct object** receives the action of a verb. | ▶ Annette called **me** before she came over. |
| ▶ An **indirect object** is used between the verb and the direct object. It tells *to whom* or *for whom* or *to what* or *for what* something was done. | ▶ The teacher gave **Lashonda** a pencil. |

**Write whether the underlined word is a direct object or an indirect object.**

1. My brother sent <u>me</u> a postcard from Russia.

   _____

2. The Kremlin holds valuable <u>artifacts</u> of Russia's past.

   _____

3. He brought me home some <u>rubles</u>, which are Russian

   money. _____

4. The Bolshoi Theater gave the audience a wonderful

   <u>performance</u>. _____

5. The tour guide showed <u>us</u> Lenin's tomb. _____

6. Olga made her family <u>borscht</u> for dinner. _____

**▶ Direct and Indirect Objects**

## Practice

**Circle the direct object and underline the indirect object if the sentence contains one.**

1. Our class watched a movie about Russia.

2. We saw tourists walking on Red Square.

3. Miss Williams read us a story about Peter the Great.

4. Mr. Silakov gave us a lecture on Russian history.

5. He brought the class a dessert called blini.

6. He also showed pictures of Moscow.

7. We made Mr. Silakov a thank-you card written in Russian.

## Proofread

**Rewrite the following sentences to shorten them and give them an indirect object.**

1. The boy sold a subway map to me because we were lost.

   _____

2. A man selling flowers gave better directions to us.

   _____

3. I wrote my address in Russian for Dimitri.

   _____

4. He presented bread and salt to us at the door as a sign of welcome.

   _____

5. Yura offered sausage and cheese to Vladimir and me.

   _____

**UNIT 4** Making a New Nation • **Lesson 5** *The Master Spy of Yorktown*

# Developing Persuasive Writing

When you write persuasively, you write with the goal of changing the way your readers think or act regarding a problem or issue.

### Rule

▶ To write persuasively, you should list your reasons in order of importance, from least to most persuasive.

▶ In persuasive writing the author often states his or her *opinion* and then reinforces that opinion with *facts*. An author may also choose to use language and reasons that appeal to readers' *emotions*.

▶ Persuasive writing may be organized by *asking and answering a question*. The question should involve the readers, and the answer should include facts and reasons that persuade the reader.

### Example

▶ Dog owners should not tie up their dogs and leave them outside. First, dogs that are tied up bark and disturb the neighbors. Second, and most important, dogs should be walked or allowed daily supervised runs so they can get proper exercise.

 **Try It!**   In persuasive writing, writers state a personal *opinion* that they reinforce with *facts* (not more opinions). For each item, write *F* for fact and *O* for opinion.

_____ 1. Everybody in the U. S. should have a computer.

_____ 2. People use computers to communicate.

_____ 3. Programs on computers help teach school subjects.

_____ 4. Children should spend no more than one hour per day using computers.

▶ **Developing Persuasive Writing**

**Practice**

**WRITER'S CRAFT**

Persuasive writing may appeal to *reason,* or to the way the audience thinks, by using facts, examples, and expert opinions. It may also appeal to *emotion,* or the way the audience feels, by using language and reasons that have emotional appeal. For each aim and audience below, write *E* for emotion or *R* for reason to show the approach it should use to persuade.

_____ 5. A letter sent home to school families asking them to support a fundraiser that helps families without adequate food and shelter.

_____ 6. A letter sent to the town supervisor asking that a side road be closed to traffic during a parade.

_____ 7. A report for your teacher on why space exploration should increase.

_____ 8. A poster created to inspire school spirit for an upcoming basketball game.

_____ 9. A paragraph encouraging people to wash hands to prevent illness.

10. Write a persuasive paragraph that appeals to reason about something that is important to you. In parentheses, label your opinion (O) and also any facts (F) and emotional appeals (E) that you use. Remember to list your reasons in order of importance.

_____

_____

_____

_____

# Fact and Opinion

**Focus**   Nonfiction texts may include both facts and opinions. Readers must be careful not to assume that all the information included in a text is factual.

> ▶ A **fact** is a statement that can be verified or tested. It can be cross-referenced, checked in other sources. It is reported in the same way by any number of observers or sources.
>
> ▶ An **opinion** cannot be verified or tested. Opinions can be supported by facts, but they cannot be proven. In addition, sources may disagree on opinions.

## Identify

Skim the selection "Shh! We're Writing the Constitution" and identify examples of fact and opinion to write in the spaces below. Under the opinion, write the facts that support it. Under the fact, write sources that could be cross-referenced to verify it.

Opinion: _____

_____

Page: _____   Paragraph: _____

Supporting Facts: _____

_____

Fact: _____

Page: _____   Paragraph: _____

Cross-Referenced in: _____

_____

**UNIT 4** Making a New Nation • **Lesson 6** *Shh! We're Writing the Constitution*

## Practice and Apply

Imagine you work for the local newspaper as a reviewer. You have just been given the assignment to review "Shh! We're Writing the Constitution." In your review, you will need to include a summary of the selection, as well as your opinion about it. Write your review in the space below. Then, exchange reviews with a classmate. Identify in your classmate's paper the sentences that contain facts and those that contain opinions.

_____

_____

_____

_____

_____

_____

_____

_____

_____

_____

_____

_____

_____

_____

**UNIT 4** Making a New Nation • **Lesson 6** *Shh! We're Writing the Constitution*

# Contractions, Negatives, and Double Negatives

| **Rule** | **Example** |
|---|---|
| ▶ A **contraction** is formed by combining two words, omitting one or more letters, and replacing the letters with an apostrophe. | ▶ Jamie said he **isn't** going tonight. **Don't** leave without me. |
| ▶ You can express the idea of *no* or *not* by using a **negative word.** Some negative words include *never, nobody, none, no one,* and *nothing*. A **double negative** occurs when two negative words are used to express a single idea. | ▶ **Incorrect:** I never saw no one there. **Correct:** I never saw anyone there. |

**Write a contraction made from the words in parentheses.**

1. _____ space flight interesting? (Is not)

2. _____ it be amazing to travel to another planet? (Would not)

3. I _____ aware that a spacecraft needs to reach a speed of about 17,500 miles per hour to get into orbit. (was not)

4. _____ that seem impossible? (Does not)

5. I _____ been to a space shuttle launching, but I would really enjoy it. (have not)

6. _____ you come with me? (Will not)

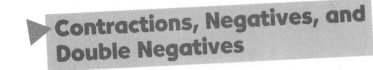

**Practice**

Contractions, Negatives, and Double Negatives

**Rewrite these sentences to eliminate double negatives and make the subjects and verbs agree.**

**1.** This book isn't no good.

_____

**2.** It doesn't say nothing about Yosemite National Park.

_____

**3.** I hadn't never thought of looking in that book.

_____

**Proofread**

**Cross out the incorrect word and write the correct word above it if one is needed. Form contractions when possible.**

I have not seen no place as beautiful as Yellowstone National Park. Although the idea to set aside the land was proposed in 1870, it was not until 1872 that President Grant signed the bill making Yellowstone the first national park. Is not it amazing that people come from all over the world to see our parks? Before I went there, I had not never seen a moose. If I had not traveled there this summer, I wouldn't have had no idea what a geyser looks like. Do you not want to go there now?

**GRAMMAR AND USAGE**

# Outlining

An outline is a plan that lists the ideas and subtopics of expository writing.

| **Rule** | **Example** |
|---|---|
| | *Computers* |
| ▶ A title stating the writing topic should be at the top of every outline. | ▶ I. How computers help people communicate |
| ▶ Use your important ideas or note card headings as the main topics for an outline. Number each main topic with a Roman numeral (I, II, III). | A. Computers are used for sending e-mail.<br>B. Computers are used for writing articles, stories, and school reports. |
| ▶ Divide main topics into subtopics. Under each main topic, indent and number each subtopic with a capital letter (A, B, C). | C. Special computers for people with disabilities |
| ▶ If subtopics require further division, indent under each subtopic and number the smaller subtopics with Arabic numerals (1, 2, 3, etc.). | 1. People who cannot speak type messages that translate into speech.<br>2. People who cannot type speak into computers that convert speech into writing. |

 **Try It!**   Write (S) subtopic or (M) main topic for an outline titled *Forests of the World*.

1. Types of trees in the Guatemalan rain forest. _____

2. Temperate forests _____

3. The rain forest canopy _____

4. Climate of the temperate forest _____

5. Tropical rain forests _____

**UNIT 4** Making a New Nation • **Lesson 6** *Shh! We're Writing the Constitution*

▶ Outlining

**Practice**

**6.** Complete the following outline by adding Roman numerals, capital letters, and Arabic numerals.

**Hurricanes**

_____ Types of hurricanes

_____ Mild hurricanes

_____ Dangerous hurricanes

_____ Mitch

_____ Andrew

**7.** Add the missing main topics and subtopics.

Winter, Build self-esteem, Track and Field, Swimming, Speed skating, Provide high-profile events for athletes with disabilities, Some major events

**The Special Olympics**

I. The goals of the Special Olympics

A. _____

B. _____

II. _____

A. Summer

1. _____

2. _____

B. _____

1. Figure skating

2. _____

WRITER'S CRAFT

# Parallelism

Use **parallelism** to add variety, smoothness, and clarity to your writing. When you use parallelism, you combine words or parts of sentences that are the same part of speech.

| **Rule** | **Example** |
|---|---|
| ▶ Parallelism often lists items in a series. Be consistent with each part of speech used in the series. Nouns go with nouns, adjectives go with adjectives, and verbs go with verbs. | ▶ She ate, studied, and slept last night. (Each item is a verb.) |
| ▶ Parallelism combines parts of sentences containing the same part of speech with conjunctions such as *either/or*, *neither/nor*, and *not only/but also*. | ▶ Neither the groundhogs nor the squirrels like to see our dog. The groundhogs not only decided to make our yard their home, but they also decided to raise their young under our shed. |
| ▶ Parallelism combines the same types of phrases or clauses. | ▶ School closed early today to allow the bus drivers time to beat the storm, to give walkers time to call their parents, and to ensure everyone's safety. (The sentence combines infinitive phrases.) |

 **Try It!** **Draw a line through the item that does not belong with the part of speech used for the other items in the series.**

1. He decorated his bicycle with beads, buttons, colorful shells, and painted.

2. Daring, comical, barked, and mischievous, the puppy had lots of personality.

3. Squeaking, honking, clarinets, and trilling, the woodwind section finished their warm-up.

**UNIT 4** **Making a New Nation • Lesson 6** *Shh! We're Writing the Constitution*

 **Parallelism**

## Practice

**Use parallelism to write sentences.**

4. Write a sentence that uses parallelism by listing the items you carry in your backpack. List items as nouns in a series.

_____

_____

5. Write a sentence that uses parallelism by listing the things you normally do after school. List activities as verbs in a series.

_____

_____

6. Write a sentence that uses parallelism by listing adjectives that describe the sky outside today. List items as adjectives, modifying *sky*.

_____

_____

7. Write a sentence about a friend that combines the same part of speech with conjunctions.

_____

_____

8. Write a paragraph that includes two examples of parallelism. Label the types of parallelism you use in parentheses (nouns in a series, parts of speech connected by a conjunction, adverb clauses, prepositional phrases).

_____

_____

WRITER'S CRAFT

# Main Idea and Details

**Focus**  Authors often build arguments by stating or implying **main ideas.** They then develop these main ideas with **details.**

> ▶ A **main idea** is the topic or subject of a selection or paragraph.
> ▶ **Details** support the main ideas by providing additional information.

## Identify

Read through "We, the People of the United States," and record three main ideas below. After each main idea, include at least two supporting details you found in the text.

Main Idea: _____

Supporting Details: _____

_____

_____

Main Idea: _____

Supporting Details: _____

_____

_____

Main Idea: _____

Supporting Details: _____

_____

_____

▶ **Main Idea and Details**

## Practice

Write in outline form below a main idea related to Making a New Nation and three details that support the main idea.

I. _____

    A. _____

    B. _____

    C. _____

## Apply

Using the outline you made above, construct a brief essay about your chosen topic. Be sure you directly state the main idea and include details that support it.

_____

_____

_____

_____

_____

_____

_____

_____

_____

_____

_____

**COMPREHENSION**

# Review

## Types of Sentences

Write *simple*, *compound*, or *complex* to tell the type of sentence.

1. _____ Thirty-nine men signed the Constitution, and 56 signed the Declaration of Independence.

2. _____ The Declaration of Independence is on display in the National Archives Building.

3. _____ James Madison, who became President of the United States, signed the Constitution.

## Subject-Verb Agreement

Write the correct past tense form of each verb in a sentence.

4. write _____

5. swing _____

6. fly _____

## Misused Words

Circle the correct word for each sentence.

7. I  **can   may**   do 100 sit-ups.

8. Please  **set   sit**   the water bottle over there.

9. She likes to  **lie   lay**   down after exercising.

10. My sister works out more often  **than   then**   I do.

**UNIT 4** Making a New Nation • **Lesson 7** *We, the People of the United States*

## Comparative and Superlative Adjectives and Adverbs

Write the comparative and superlative form of each adjective or adverb.

11. hard _____ _____

12. loudly _____ _____

13. badly _____ _____

14. far _____ _____

## Direct and Indirect Objects

**Circle the direct objects and underline the indirect objects in the following sentences.**

15. Jake gave his mother a flower.

16. I bought her a glass vase.

17. Alli got Mom a picture for her birthday.

18. We saved Lane a seat at the restaurant.

## Contractions, Negatives, and Double Negatives

**Write a contraction on the line that best completes each sentence.**

19. _____ the nickname of Maine the Pine Tree State?

20. I _____ remember the nickname of Florida.

21. _____ you studying the fifty states?

22. _____ you like to know which state is known as the North Star State?

**GRAMMAR AND USAGE**

# Sentence Variety

| Rule | Example |
| --- | --- |
| ▶ Avoid repeating the same word over and over. Use exact words (synonyms) to replace common and overused words.<br><br>▶ Vary the beginning of sentences to add interest to writing. | ▶ *Before:* It was nice of you to walk with me on this nice day.<br>*Improved:* It was thoughtful of you to walk with me on this beautiful day.<br><br>▶ *Before:* We built the tree house. We added carpet. We added chairs. We had a hideaway.<br>*Improved:* After we built the tree house, we added carpet, and even chairs. We had the perfect hideaway. |
| ▶ Use appositives to improve short, explanatory sentences. | ▶ *Before:* My friend is Dr. Ring. She used to work for Doctors without Borders.<br>*Improved:* My friend, Dr. Ring, used to work for Doctors without Borders. |
| ▶ Use sentences of different lengths to improve the rhythm and flow of writing. | |

 **Label the italicized word(s) by writing *exact word* or *appositive.***

1. Our dog, *an Irish Terrier,* has red fur. _____

2. We saw his book collection and *spotted* some of our

   favorite books. _____

3. He *informed* us that adventure stories were his favorites

   and said we could borrow some. _____

**UNIT 4**  Making a New Nation • **Lesson 7**  *We the People of the United States*

► **Sentence Variety**

## Practice

**4.** Draw a line to show the best way to improve the sentences below.

| | |
|---|---|
| She likes cats. She has several. She takes in strays. | Use an appositive. |
| It is Friday. I'm excited. We will bowl. | Vary the sentence beginnings. |
| Ari is a Girl Scout. She will help plant trees. | Vary the sentence lengths. |
| We ran toward the goal. Sunil ran there first. Instead, we ran away. | Use exact words to replace an overused word. |

**Sometimes you can use more than one technique to improve sentence variety. Fix the sentences below by using exact words, appositives, and varied sentence lengths and beginnings.**

**5.** Our teacher is sick. The assistant principal is teaching us today. Her name is Ms. Ortega.

_____

_____

**6.** Monday was cold and rainy. Tuesday was dry and cold. Wednesday was warmer. Thursday was very warm and sunny.

_____

_____

_____

**WRITER'S CRAFT**

# Organizing Persuasive Writing

| Rule | Example |
|---|---|
| ▶ Reasons should be listed in order of importance, from least to most persuasive. | |
| ▶ Persuasive writing may be organized by asking and answering a question. The question should involve readers, and the answer should include the facts, reasons, and examples that persuade readers. | ▶ Why should our school recycle? First, it teaches students and adults the importance of taking care of the environment in their daily lives. Second, it reduces the amount of trash that must be burned in the county incinerator. Third and most important, by reusing materials we reduce the need to create new ones. |
| ▶ Persuasive writing can be organized by presenting a problem and offering one or more solutions. | ▶ This is how we can help solve the problem of crowded roads in our city. People can use bicycles, share rides with other people, and most important, they can support the proposed metro rail project. It would provide train transportation from suburban neighborhoods to downtown. |

 **Try It!**   **Write either *problem/solution* or *question/answer* to show how you would organize persuasive writing reports on both of the following topics.**

1. Your school library needs more reference and nonfiction books for students to use as resources for reports.

_____

2. People need to understand why art is important.

_____

**UNIT 4** **Making a New Nation** • **Lesson 7** *We the People of the United States*

**Organizing Persuasive Writing**

**Practice**

Persuasive writing uses reasons to persuade readers to act on or adopt the point of view presented. Write *fact, example,* or *opinion* to label the type of reason that each sentence below is.

3. _____ Scientists who study sleep say most adults need eight hours per night.

4. _____ The layer of fat underneath a polar bear's dense fur is 4 inches thick.

5. _____ It takes 35 days for emperor penguin eggs to hatch.

6. _____ For instance, my grandfather remembers more things from his childhood than my father remembers from his.

7. _____ The building engineer says that the structure will support a rock-climbing wall.

8. _____ A good illustration of this is the condensation that forms on the bathroom mirror after taking a shower.

9. Write a persuasive paragraph. Organize it by asking and answering a question or by presenting a problem and providing solutions. Describe the method that you use in parentheses at the beginning of your paragraph. List your reasons in order of importance.

_____

_____

_____

_____

**WRITER'S CRAFT**

# Drawing Conclusions

**Focus** When writers don't include all the information about a character or event in a story, good readers **draw conclusions** using information in the text.

> **Drawing conclusions** means putting together information from the text to make a statement about a character or event. The conclusion won't be stated directly, but it should be supported by information in the the text.

## Identify

Look through "Sacagawea's Journey." What conclusions did you come to about people or events in the selection? Find places in the text that helped you draw conclusions.

Page: _____

Conclusion: _____

Information that supports the conclusion: _____

_____

_____

_____

Page: _____

Conclusion: _____

Information that supports the conclusion: _____

_____

_____

_____

**UNIT 5** Going West • **Lesson 1** *Sacagawea's Journey*

### Practice

**Drawing Conclusions**

Think about an important discovery in the American West that you might want a reader to draw a conclusion about. First, decide what conclusion you want the reader to draw. Then, write some clues that will help the reader come to that conclusion.

The discovery: _____

Conclusion: _____

Clues: _____

_____

_____

_____

### Apply

Use the above clues to write a paragraph about the discovery you chose. Read your paragraph to a classmate and have him or her draw a conclusion about the discovery. Discuss what information in the paragraph the conclusion was based on.

_____

_____

_____

_____

_____

_____

_____

COMPREHENSION

**UNIT 5** Going West • **Lesson I** *Sacagawea's Journey*

# Fragments

| Rule | Example |
|---|---|
| ▶ A **sentence** is a group of words that expresses a complete thought. Always capitalize the first word of a sentence. | ▶ Our first president was George Washington. |
| ▶ A **fragment** does not express a complete thought. It may be missing a subject, a predicate, or both. | ▶ led the American forces through the Revolution *(missing a subject)*<br><br>His victory over the British at Yorktown in 1781 *(missing a predicate)*<br><br>on the night of December 25, 1776 *(missing both)* |

**Write *Yes* in the blank before each group of words that is a sentence. Write *No* if it is a fragment.**

1. _____ His favorite sport.

2. _____ Ice hockey was first played in Canada in the 1830s.

3. _____ By the 1880s, the first professional teams.

4. _____ Players, wearing padding on the chest, shoulders, arms, and shins.

5. _____ Pucks are knocked across the ice.

6. _____ Can shoot the puck up to 110 miles per hour.

**Fragments**

## Practice

**Write whether the following fragments are missing a subject, a predicate, or both.**

7. polar bears in the North and South Poles _____

8. have adapted to the cold weather _____

9. the polar bear, which swims very well _____

10. eat seals, fish, birds, and small mammals _____

11. in a den of ice and snow _____

## Proofread

**Join all the fragments in the following paragraph with complete sentences. Draw three lines under letters that should be capitalized.**

at the southern end of Earth's axis, lying in Antarctica, is the South Pole. not the same as the magnetic South Pole. the south pole, at an elevation of some 9,300 feet above sea level. it has six months of complete daylight and six months of total darkness each year. ice thickness is 8,850 feet. first reached by the Norwegian explorer Roald Amundsen on Dec. 14, 1911. the South Pole was reached the following year by the British explorer Robert F. Scott. and again in 1929 by the American explorer Richard E. Byrd.

GRAMMAR AND USAGE

# Main Idea and Details

**Focus** Writers usually include a **main idea** in every paragraph of their writing. These main ideas are supported by **details** that make up the rest of the paragraph.

> A **main idea** is the most important idea in a paragraph, a passage, or an entire work.
> ▶ In paragraphs, the main idea is usually stated in a topic sentence.
> ▶ The main idea of a larger section of text or an entire work sometimes must be inferred.
> ▶ The other sentences in the paragraph include details that support the main idea.

## Identify

Read the fourth paragraph on page 425 in "Buffalo Hunt." Identify the topic sentence of the paragraph and the details that support this main idea.

Topic Sentence: _____

_____

_____

Supporting Details: _____

_____

_____

_____

_____

**UNIT 5** Going West • **Lesson 2** *Buffalo Hunt*

**Main Idea and Details**

### Practice

Think about some of the things you just learned about buffalo and the Native Americans. Choose one thing you want to say about what you learned. Write that as your main idea. Then write three details that support your main idea.

**Main Idea:** _____

**Detail 1:** _____

**Detail 2:** _____

**Detail 3:** _____

### Apply

Use the above main idea and details to write a paragraph about the Native Americans and buffalo. Make sure your paragraph states your main idea in a topic sentence. When you are finished, read your paragraph to a classmate and see if he or she can identify the main idea of the paragraph.

_____

_____

_____

_____

_____

_____

_____

_____

**COMPREHENSION**

**UNIT 5** Going West • **Lesson 2** *Buffalo Hunt*

# Commas with Introductory Phrases

A comma should follow a long introductory phrase.

| **Rule** | **Example** |
|---|---|
| ▶ Set off two or more prepositional phrases with a comma. | ▶ **In the summer of 2000,** our family went to Washington, D.C. |
| ▶ Set off a long prepositional phrase with a comma. | ▶ **Of all America's tourist attractions,** Washington, D.C., is one of the most popular. |
| ▶ Set off a participial phrase at the beginning of a sentence. | ▶ **Walking along the mall,** we saw several museums. |

**Add a comma to each sentence below to separate an introductory phrase from the main sentence.**

1. Beneath the bright lights of the big city many people rose to fame.

2. Every four years a new president is inaugurated.

3. Agreeing to cooperate under a new government the colonies gave up some of their independence.

4. Of all periods in American history I like the Civil War era best.

5. At the request of his fellow committee members Thomas Jefferson wrote the first draft of the Constitution.

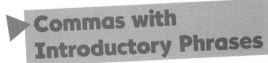
Commas with Introductory Phrases

**Practice**

**Insert commas where they are needed.**

6. Agreeing that a second meeting was needed the representatives drew the first meeting to a close.

7. In July 1776 the Declaration of Independence was signed.

8. At the beginning of the Constitution the Bill of Rights reinforces the guarantee of individual rights.

9. Living in a free country we have the right to vote.

**Proofread**

**Rewrite the word groups to connect the introductory phrases to the main sentences.**

10. Beneath the stars of his native Italy. Galileo set up his telescope.

   _____

   _____

11. Peering under the lid of the piano. We saw how the hammers made music.

   _____

   _____

12. Above the limbs of the mighty sequoia. The eagle glided through the air.

   _____

   _____

MECHANICS

# Sequence

**Focus** When writers tell a story or explain a process, they must express the **sequence** in which events occur.

> **Sequence** is indicated by time words and order words.
> ▶ Words such as *earlier, later, now, then, morning, day, evening,* and *night* indicate **time.**
> ▶ Words such as *first, second, last, following, next, after, during,* and *finally* indicate **order.**

## Identify

Look through "The Journal of Wong Ming-Chung." Choose one of the diary entries and summarize the sequence of events on the lines provided. Be sure to include time words and order words.

Page: _____

Entry date: _____

Events in sequence: _____

_____

_____

_____

_____

_____

_____

_____

_____

▶ Sequence

**Practice and Apply**

Think about the things you have done so far today. Make a list of those things, placing them in the proper sequence.

_____

_____

_____

_____

_____

_____

Now, write a paragraph describing your day so far. Use time words and order words to express the sequence of events in your day. _____

_____

_____

_____

_____

_____

_____

_____

COMPREHENSION

# Punctuation and Capitalization in Friendly Letters

| **Rule** | **Example** |
|---|---|
| ▶ A friendly letter begins with a heading. Street names, months, and place names in the heading should be capitalized. Place a comma between the city and the state and also between the date and the year. There is no comma between the state and the ZIP code. | ▶ 21 **M**ain **S**treet **D**ayton, OH 45403 **S**eptember 17, 2003 |
| ▶ The greeting and closing of a friendly letter begin with a capital letter and end with a comma. Capitalize all proper nouns. | ▶ **D**ear **A**unt **M**ary, Thank you for the sweater. It fits perfectly and is my favorite color. I hope to see you soon. Your niece, Misty |

 **Circle any letters that should be capitalized in the following friendly letter. Insert any missing commas.**

418 fleur street
belleville WA 98417
july 10 2002

dear aunt Lois
Thank you for sending me the Virginia state quarter. I've been looking for one for a month!

your nephew
Brian

Comprehension and Language Arts Skills

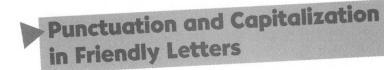

## Punctuation and Capitalization in Friendly Letters

### Practice

**Write the missing parts of the letter below.**

_____

_____

_____

_____

    I enjoyed working with you at the craft meeting last night. You are always welcome to share my supplies. See you at our next meeting!

_____

Elizabeth

### Proofread

**Draw three lines under each letter that should be capitalized, and add or delete commas as needed.**

514 High street
centerville TN, 48829
September, 12 2001

dear Jen
    You were very thoughtful to send me the book about horses. How did you know that is my favorite hobby? I hope you visit again soon. You are welcome anytime.

              sincerely
              Margaret

MECHANICS

# Structure of a Personal Letter

> **Rule**
> ▶ In the upper right corner, include a **heading** containing your address and the date.
> ▶ Include a **salutation**—the word *Dear*—followed by the name of the person receiving the letter and a comma. Line up the salutation with the left margin, two lines below the heading.
> ▶ Include a **body,** the things you say in the letter, two lines below the salutation. Indent every paragraph of the body.
> ▶ Write the **closing** two lines below the body in line with the left margin. Capitalize just the first word and follow the last word with a comma.
> ▶ Add your **signature** (your signed name) under the closing.

## Try It!

**1.** Draw a line to match each friendly letter part with its example.

Body                    *Ian Halliday*

Salutation              578 Gladys Ave.
                        Augusta, ME 00467
                        October 17, 2001

Signature               Sincerely,

Closing                 Last week I made an amazing
                        bike course in the meadow in
                        back of our house.

Heading                 Dear Zechariah,

**UNIT 5** Going West • **Lesson 3** *The Journal of Wong Ming-Chung*

▶ **Structure of a Personal Letter**

**Practice**

**2.** Label the parts of this personal letter.

330 Whispering Pines Rd. _____
Baldwin, Michigan 49789

August 29, 2001 _____

Dear Makayla, _____

   It definitely is a lot quieter in northern Michigan than it is in
Southfield. I really miss you and the other girls, but I am

starting to make some new friends. _____
   You wouldn't believe all of the wildlife up here. I see deer
all the time, and yesterday I even saw a bear. I haven't made
friends with any of them yet!
   The weather up here this summer was warm, but not
always hot enough for swimming. School will be starting
soon. Write back and wish me luck.

Yours truly, _____

*Alissa* _____

**3.** Write a one-paragraph personal letter to someone you
   haven't seen for a while. Include each part of a personal
   letter and label it.

_____

_____

_____

_____

_____

_____

**WRITER'S CRAFT**

# Punctuation and Capitalization in Business Letters

| **Rule** | **Example** |
|---|---|
| ▶ A business letter begins with a heading in the upper right-hand corner. Place a comma between the city and state, and the date and year. Capitalize the proper nouns. | ▶ 1354 Eastland Drive<br>San Diego, CA 92138<br>April 8, 2003 |
| ▶ In the inside address, also capitalize the recipient's name, his or her title, and the company's name. | ▶ Mr. Jorge Alvarez<br>Vice President of Customer Relations<br>Bayview Surf School<br>114 Bayview Circle<br>San Diego, CA  92138 |
| ▶ The greeting and closing are capitalized. A colon follows the greeting, and a comma follows the closing. Include your signature between the closing and your typed name. | ▶ Dear Mr. Alvarez:<br><br>Sincerely,<br>*Minka Larouge*<br>Minka Larouge |

 **Try It!**   Write the missing parts of the letter below.

_____

   The radio I bought at your store no longer works. I had it for only three weeks before it broke. I am wondering what I need to do to receive a replacement. Thank you for your time.

_____

*John Chang*
John Chang

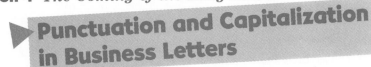

**Punctuation and Capitalization in Business Letters**

**Practice**

**Circle any letters that should be capitalized and insert commas where needed.**

> 627 Ambrose street
> prescott AZ 86743
> july 8 2002

Mr. Trenton Anderson
president
Fine Clothing, Inc.
85 easton street
apex, NC 27502

**Proofread**

**Draw three lines under each letter that should be capitalized. Delete or add punctuation as needed.**

> 14 central street
> phoenix, AZ, 84345
> october 19 2002

Ms. elaine olson
vice president
AFR Company
83 walnut street
portsmouth PA 29438

Dear Ms. olson,
   I am very interested in the products you offer. Please send me a list of your computer games. Thank you very much.

> sincerely
> *Brent Armstrong*
> Brent Armstrong

MECHANICS

# Structure of a Business Letter

**Rule**

▶ Include a **heading**—your own address and also the date.
▶ Include an **inside address**—the name of the person who is to receive the letter. After the person's name, add a comma and title (if there is one).
▶ Use a **salutation,** or greeting. Put a colon after it.
▶ In the **body,** briefly and politely include what you want to say. Do not indent.
▶ Add the **closing** two lines below the body by the left margin. Capitalize only the first word of a two-word closing and use a comma after the second word.
▶ Add your **signature** (handwritten name) two lines below the closing.

## Try It!

1. Draw a line to match each business letter part with its example.

Body                 Dear Ms. Cavan:

Salutation           Charlotte Cavan, Program Coordinator
                     The Academy of Natural Sciences
                     1901 Benjamin Franklin Pkwy.
                     Philadelphia, PA 19103

Heading              I am writing to learn how our class
                     can adopt a bat.

Closing

Inside Address       Parkway Terrace Apts. #309
                     2100 Pennsylvania Ave.
                     Philadelphia, PA 19120
                     February 15, 2002

Signature            Yours truly,

▶ **Structure of a Business Letter**

**Practice**

**2.** What is missing from this business letter? _____

112 Logan Rd.
Watertown, MA 02472
May 17, 2001

To Whom It May Concern:

I am writing in response to your park planning contest. Please
find enclosed my diagram of what I think the future park
should look like. I think you will find that it meets the needs
of city residents of all ages. I look forward to learning the
results of the contest.

*Sylvia Formigoni*

Sylvia Formigoni

**3.** Write a brief, imaginary business letter asking a company
   that makes lockers to include an idea you have for
   improving the design of lockers. Use this made-up name for
   the salutation and inside address. For the other four
   business letter parts, use your own name and ideas.

Vincent Vanderveen, Chief Engineer
Lockers Unlimited, Inc.
438 Whitehorse Rd.
Cedar Rapids, IA  56703

_____

_____

_____

_____

_____

WRITER'S CRAFT

# Making Inferences

**Focus**  Writers do not always provide complete information about story elements. Therefore, readers **make inferences** in order to better understand the story elements.

> To **make an inference:**
> ► look for clues in the story that tell about a character, a thing, or an event.
> ► use your prior knowledge to interpret the clues.

## Identify

Read page 465, paragraph 5, of "Old Yeller and the Bear."

What inference can you make about Travis from this sentence? "She said that if he ever told a bigger whopper than the ones I used to tell, she had to hear it."

_____

## Practice

Skim "Old Yeller and the Bear" for clues about Mama's personality. Use your prior knowledge to make an inference about Mama based on these clues.

**Clues:** _____

_____

**Prior knowledge:** _____

_____

**Inference:** _____

_____

**UNIT 5**  Going West • **Lesson 5**  *Old Yeller and the Bear*

### Apply

Use your prior knowledge to make inferences based on each of the following sentences.

### Example:

You look out the window and see people wearing heavy coats, hats, and gloves.

**Inference:** *It is cold outside.*

1. You hear pots and pans banging in the kitchen, and you start to smell something good.

   **Inference:** _____

2. Fred didn't feel good yesterday, and he is not at school today.

   **Inference:** _____

3. Every time Susan goes to Ted's house, his cat jumps into her lap and purrs.

   **Inference:** _____

4. The dog gobbles up the beef treats you give him but spits out the chicken ones.

   **Inference:** _____

5. At a restaurant, the child at the next table is blowing out candles on a big cake.

   **Inference:** _____

COMPREHENSION

# Commas with Independent and Subordinate Clauses

A comma is used between two independent clauses and after a subordinate clause that begins a sentence.

| **Rule** | **Example** |
|---|---|
| ▶ An independent clause expresses a complete thought. A coordinating conjunction and a comma may connect two related independent clauses. Coordinating conjunctions include *and, but, or, so, yet,* and *for.* | ▶ Patty runs track, **and** Pam pole vaults.<br><br>I want to join them, **but** I don't have time. |
| ▶ A subordinate clause has a subject and a predicate but does not express a complete thought. Put a comma after a subordinate clause that begins a sentence. Some subordinating conjunctions include *as, because, if, unless,* and *when.* | ▶ **When you arrive,** let me know.<br><br>**Unless we vote,** our voices will not be heard. |

 **Try It!** Draw a slash where the first independent clause ends. Draw another slash where the second independent clause begins.

1. Each tennis player has a racket, and points are scored by hitting the ball over the net.

2. The ball must then be returned, but it doesn't have to bounce off the court first.

3. The rubber balls that were first used didn't work well when they got wet, so a flannel covering was invented.

4. The pressure inside the balls changes in different temperatures, so the balls used in matches are refrigerated.

**UNIT 5** Going West • **Lesson 5** *Old Yeller and the Bear*

**Commas with Independent and Subordinate Clauses**

**Practice**

**Rewrite each pair as one sentence. Begin with the subordinate clause using the word in parentheses to start.**

**5.** She was late. Maria didn't get to vote. (because)

_____

**6.** A commercial is successful. People remember the product and buy it. (if)

_____

_____

**7.** The red panda looks like a bear. It is a raccoon. (although)

_____

_____

**8.** You attend the book fair. You will have more information about the books we offer. (after)

_____

_____

**Proofread**

**Use subordinating conjunctions to combine four sets of sentences. Add commas as necessary. Draw a slash through letters that should be lowercase.**

You take clothes out of the dryer. You can hear the crackle of electricity. Atoms have a charge of electricity. They act in interesting ways. Objects made of different substances rub together. The atoms become electrically charged. I walked on carpeting yesterday. I felt a spark of electricity!

MECHANICS

**UNIT 5** Going West • **Lesson 5** *Old Yeller and the Bear*

# Tone of a Personal Letter

Most personal letters have a friendly, informal tone. The tone that you use in a personal letter reflects your attitude toward the subject. Carefully choose words that communicate the tone you wish to achieve.

### Rule

▶ Let your purpose guide you as you write. For example, if you are writing with the specific aim of telling about a recent personal adventure, use strong verbs, suspense, and surprise to create a tone that shows your own interest and involves your reader in your adventure.

▶ Be aware of who your audience is. Whether you are writing to just one person or several people, you will want to use the tone that is appropriate for them. For example, a letter written to a younger sibling would have a much more casual tone than a polite letter written to a grandparent.

 **Try It!**

**1.** Write the letter to match the tone with the specific aim.

**Aim**

_____ a letter telling a grandparent about a pet that died

_____ a letter telling a cousin that your family is coming to visit

_____ a letter written from camp telling your parents that you miss them

_____ a letter written to a friend about an amusing story you heard

**Tone**

**A.** light, funny

**B.** open, emotional

**C.** polite, sad

**D.** excited, informative

**▶ Tone of a Personal Letter**

**WRITER'S CRAFT**

**Practice**

**Describe the tone you would use for each of the following.**

2. You want to tell a friend who moved to another state everything that has happened in your life since he or she moved.

_____

3. You want to share a list of your top ten videos of the year with a friend.

_____

4. You wish to comfort a neighbor whose grandparent has died.

_____

5. You are responding to an aunt who wrote you a letter with questions about your interests.

_____

6. You are writing a great–grandparent and have a list of questions about what it was like growing up during the Great Depression.

_____

7. Write a paragraph that could be included in the body of a friendly letter sent to a friend. Write about what you like about him or her. In parentheses, describe your tone.

_____

_____

_____

_____

_____

# Fact and Opinion

**Focus**   Good writers use both facts and opinions in their writing. A good reader can tell one from the other.

> ▶ **Facts** are details that can be proven true or false.
> ▶ **Opinions** are what people think. They cannot be proven true or false.

## Identify

Skim "Bill Pickett: Rodeo-Ridin' Cowboy" for examples in which the author states facts and opinions. Write the page number, identify each example as a fact or opinion, and write the example. Be sure to find examples of both.

**1.** Page: _____     Fact or opinion? _____

Example: _____

_____

**2.** Page: _____     Fact or opinion? _____

Example: _____

_____

**3.** Page: _____     Fact or opinion? _____

Example: _____

_____

**4.** Page: _____     Fact or opinion? _____

Example: _____

_____

**UNIT 5**  Going West • **Lesson 6**  *Bill Pickett: Rodeo Ridin' Cowboy*

▶ **Fact and Opinion**

### Practice

Read each sentence below and tell whether it is a fact or an opinion.

**1.** Covered wagons were the best mode of transportation for pioneers. _____

**2.** As Americans began to explore the land out west, they found it inhabited by Native Americans. _____

**3.** Lewis and Clark were among the first to journey west on a scientific expedition. _____

**4.** A new life in a new land was worth the slow, steady trek pioneers made across country. _____

**5.** When Bill Pickett's two cousins came to visit, they bragged about their life on the trail. _____

**6.** A cowboy's life was a good life. _____

### Apply

Explorers, hunters, naturalists, cowboys, and other adventurers traveled west. Select one of these adventurers and write a paragraph about his or her travels. You may want to do some research to get factual information. Include both facts and opinions in your paragraph.

_____

_____

_____

_____

_____

_____

**COMPREHENSION**

Comprehension and Language Arts Skills

# Commas with Quotation Marks, Appositives, Interrupters, and Introductory Words

| **Rule** | **Example** |
|---|---|
| ▶ A comma is used to set off an appositive, a word or phrase placed next to a noun to provide extra information. | ▶ Eric's dog, **a black Lab,** took first place at the show. |
| ▶ Commas are used to set off interrupters, words or phrases that interrupt the main idea of a sentence. | ▶ Jean, **if I remember correctly,** likes dogs. |
| ▶ A comma is used to set off introductory words. | **Yes,** we won the game! |
| ▶ Use quotation marks to enclose a direct quotation. Place the end punctuation inside the closing quotation mark when it is part of the quotation. The comma before the quotation goes outside the opening quotation mark. | ▶ He asked, **"Did you like the play?"** |

 **Underline the appositive in each sentence below.**

1. My brother's car, a black convertible, is parked outside.

2. We traveled to Denali National Park, a large park in Alaska.

3. Prisana, my friend from Thailand, will be here tomorrow.

4. Have you ever picked chokecherries, a type of American wild cherry?

► **Commas with Quotation Marks, Appositives, Interrupters, and Introductory Words**

## Practice

**Place commas where they are needed.**

5. Oh can you show me the new painting?

6. No but I can if you like show you the sculpture.

7. Well this is quite a surprise.

8. Brandon said "I thought you were supposed to bring the map."

9. Yes but didn't you say "I have an extra one for you" or was I incorrect?

## Proofread

**Correct the errors in the use of commas, end marks, and quotation marks in the paragraphs below.**

"Now Andre, can you tell me the highest wind speed ever measured"? asked Mr. Martinez.

"Well was, it in the United States, " asked Andre?

"Yes it was. Do you know where in the United States"? asked Mr. Martinez.

"I believe it was in New Hampshire the, Granite State", replied Andre.

"Good for you, Andre"! exclaimed Mr. Martinez.

MECHANICS

# Cause and Effect

**Focus** Most stories revolve around several **cause-and-effect** relationships. Recognizing these relationships can help readers better understand the story.

> ▶ A **cause** is why something happened.
> ▶ An **effect** is what happened.

## Identify

Look through "McBroom the Rainmaker" and identify four effects on animals caused by the drought.

**Effect:** _____

_____

**Effect:** _____

_____

**Effect:** _____

_____

**Effect:** _____

_____

## Practice

Read the sentences below and identify the cause and effect in each one.

**1.** We spent our bus money at the mall, so we had to walk home.

   **Cause:** _____

   **Effect:** _____

**UNIT 5** Going West • **Lesson 7** *McBroom the Rainmaker*

▶**Cause and Effect**

**2.** My dad gave me five dollars because I washed the car.

Cause: _____

Effect: _____

**3.** I stayed home from school because I was sick.

Cause: _____

Effect: _____

**4.** I slipped on the ice and broke my ankle.

Cause: _____

Effect: _____

**5.** My dog started barking when he heard the doorbell ring.

Cause: _____

Effect: _____

**Apply**

Write a paragraph that includes several cause-and-effect relationships. You might use one of the sentences above as the basis of your paragraph.

_____

_____

_____

_____

_____

**COMPREHENSION**

# Review

## ► Fragments

**Write whether each fragment is missing a subject, a predicate, or both.**

**1.** his ideas about the homecoming float

_____

**2.** of all his ideas

_____

## ► Commas with Introductory Phrases and Clauses

**Rewrite the word group below as one sentence.**

**3.** Tossing the newspaper on the floor. His father jumped to answer the telephone.

_____

_____

## ► Commas and Capitalization in Friendly Letters

**Circle the letters that should be capitalized and insert any commas that are missing.**

418 main street
pittsburgh PA 34985
january 12 2002

dear Aunt amelia
   Thank you for sending me the article about sharks. It will be very useful for my research paper.

       your niece
       Carissa

▶ **Review**

## ▶ Punctuation and Capitalization in Business Letters

**Write the missing parts of the letter below.**

650 North Central Avenue

_____

_____

Mr. Kevin Colton

_____

_____

213 14th Street
Los Angeles, CA 98437

## ▶ Commas

**Rewrite each pair of sentences as one sentence.**

**4.** People go to the beach. They usually take towels.

_____

_____

**5.** Tom shopped all day. The rest of us went to the beach.

_____

_____

**Correct the use of commas, end marks, and quotation marks in the paragraph below.**

Today our geography teacher said, "Connecticut the Constitution State is on the New England coast. It was once an agricultural center. I think it's one of the most beautiful places I've ever seen. You will have to travel there someday"! he exclaimed.

GRAMMAR, USAGE, AND MECHANICS

# Structure of a Memo

A memo has its own format that is different from that of a business letter. When you a write a memo be sure to include the necessary parts.

**Rule**
▶ Centered at the top of every memo is the word *memo*.
▶ A memo heading consists of five smaller headings including **Date:, To:, From:, Subject:,** and sometimes **CC:,** each one followed by a colon.
▶ Write *CC:* before a list of everyone who will receive copies of the memo. *CC* stands for carbon copy (even though nearly all memos today are computer generated or photocopied).
▶ The author of a memo sometimes writes his or her initials after the typed name printed next to *From:* (From: Lynn Haskell *LH*
▶ Your message forms the **body** of the memo.

## Try It!

1. Write a memo heading to go with each line of information. Be sure to use a colon after each heading.

_____ January 15, 2001

_____ Siri Clark

_____ Mrs. Muster

_____ Art materials

_____ All mural committee members

> **Structure of a Memo**

**WRITER'S CRAFT**

**Practice**

**2.** This memo has none of its parts in place. Rewrite the information in memo format, including all of the necessary headings.

This memo is for July 17, 2000. It goes specifically to Kelly Compagner and Jeff Chang but everyone who works at Blue Lake State Park should get copies. It is from head ranger Aaron Furr. It is about using the new trash lids designed to keep raccoons and other animals from getting into trash containers. The latch on the lids must be snapped shut at all times in order for the containers to work properly.

Memo

_____

_____

_____

_____

_____

_____

_____

_____

_____

_____

_____

_____

# Sequence

**Focus** When writers tell a story or explain a process, they must express the order or **sequence** of events.

> Writers use **time words** and **order words** to indicate the sequence of events.
>
> ▶ Examples of time words are *earlier, later, now, then, morning, day, evening,* and *night.*
>
> ▶ Examples of order words are *first, second, last, then, following, next, after,* and *during.*

## Identify

Skim the first page of "The Story of Jumping Mouse." Write the time words and order words that indicate the sequence of events described on that page. Then, list the events in the order in which they occurred.

Time words and order words: _____

_____

Events in sequence: _____

_____

_____

_____

_____

_____

_____

**UNIT 6** Journeys and Quests • **Lesson I** *The Story of Jumping Mouse*

**Sequence**

### Practice and Apply

Think about something you know how to do, like making a sandwich. Make a list of steps needed to complete the process, placing them in the order in which they occurred.

_____

_____

_____

_____

_____

_____

Now write a paragraph describing the process. Use time words and order words to express the sequence of steps.

_____

_____

_____

_____

_____

_____

_____

COMPREHENSION

# Review

## Plural Nouns

**Write the plural form of each noun.**

**1.** man _____

**2.** goose _____

**3.** donkey _____

**4.** case _____

**5.** bench _____

**6.** dress _____

## Pronouns

**Circle the pronouns in this paragraph.**

If you travel to Dublin, Ireland, you will see that it has some amazing sights. We saw row houses, famous for their beautiful doorways. My sister enjoyed St. Stephen's Green, one of Ireland's prettiest parks. She always likes to be outdoors. I enjoyed the Irish songs at the concert in the park.

## Verbs

**Underline the action verbs in this paragraph. Circle the state of being verbs. Put brackets around the auxiliary verbs.**

Our class goes to the art museum every year. I have visited the museum many times with my family. I paint almost every day. My dad also is a very good painter. We are the only artists in the family. I attend art classes after school. Someday, my pictures will hang in a museum. I am sure of it!

**UNIT 6** Journeys and Quests • **Lesson 1** *The Story of Jumping Mouse*

▶ **Review**

▶ ## Kinds of Sentences

**Correct the punctuation in this paragraph. Draw three lines under each letter that should be capitalized at the beginning of a sentence.**

Do you know what literature is. literature is writing that is of lasting value and has strong insight into human emotions? literature is also powerful because an author can use it to express his or her ideas and beliefs. for example, many novels have been written to show the horrors of war? what an awesome responsibility it is to be an author?

▶ ## Subjects and Predicates

**Circle the simple subject and underline the simple predicate in each sentence.**

Early travelers found their way by asking directions from other travelers on the road. Their guides created the first maps by scratching rough drawings of the route in the dirt. Today, maps still show the locations of different places. However, we have many different kinds of maps. We can buy maps that cover a small area in great detail and maps that show a larger area in less detail.

**GRAMMAR, USAGE, AND MECHANICS**

Name _____ Date _____

**UNIT 6** Journeys and Quests • **Lesson 1** *The Story of Jumping Mouse*

# Variety in Writing

| Rule | Example |
|---|---|
| ▶ Avoid repeating the same word over and over. Use exact words (synonyms) to replace common and overused words. | ▶ **Before:** That was a very good jump, but it would be good if your landing were also good. <br> **Improved:** That was an excellent jump, but it would be better if you would land more gracefully. |
| ▶ Vary the beginnings of sentences to add interest to writing. | ▶ **Before:** It was a cold and rainy day. It was not what we expected. It was so wet outside. It seemed better to hold field day on another day. <br> **Improved:** The weather was much colder and rainier than we expected. Because it was so wet outside, we decided to hold field day on another day. |
| ▶ Use appositives to cut down on short, explanatory sentences. | ▶ **Before:** My dog is named Leo. He is an Irish terrier. <br> **Improved:** My dog, Leo, is an Irish terrier. |
| ▶ Use sentences of different lengths to improve the rhythm and flow of writing. | |

 **Try It!** Label the italicized word by writing *exact word* or *appositive*.

1. After we went to my friend's house and nobody was

   home, we slowly *trudged* home. _____

2. Kira Scott, *the lunch aide*, will monitor the playground

   today. _____

3. After giving us lots of old clothing, they also *donated*

   furniture. _____

Comprehension and Language Arts Skills

**UNIT 6** Journeys and Quests • **Lesson 1** *The Story of Jumping Mouse*

▶ **Variety in Writing**

**WRITER'S CRAFT**

**Practice**

**4.** Write the letter to match each sentence with the best way to improve it.

_____ We like pudding. It is good. Let's have some.

A. Use an appositive.

_____ The squirrel jumped on the feeder. The squirrel swung wildly. The squirrel scattered the seed.

B. Vary the sentence lengths.

_____ Ethan Carter is a chess player. He won his first tournament.

C. Vary the sentence beginnings.

_____ He talked about how he became an Olympic diver, and he also talked about doing well in school.

D. Use exact words to replace an overused word.

**Within a paragraph, you will often use more than one technique to improve sentence variety. Rewrite the sentences below by using exact words, appositives, varied sentence lengths, and varied beginnings.**

**5.** We saw the green blaze marking the trail and turned to the left. We saw only red blazes after that and we wondered if we were on the wrong path. We saw that we had no other choice but to backtrack.

_____

_____

_____

_____

_____

Comprehension and Language Arts Skills

# Review

## ▶ Capitalization

**Draw three lines under letters of proper nouns that should be capitalized.**

Charleston, south carolina, is a beautiful and interesting place. Founded in about 1673 on a peninsula between the ashley and cooper Rivers, charleston attracted settlers with land priced at a penny an acre. Among the many places you will want to visit are the heyward-washington House, st. michael's Church, and the confederate museum of history.

## ▶ Capitalization

**Correctly rewrite the word or words in each sentence that should be capitalized.**

**1.** My sister is a member of the girl scouts. _____

**2.** Have you read *Officer buckle and Gloria*? _____

**3.** The revolutionary war is an interesting history topic. _____

**4.** What is the magna Carta ? _____

**5.** This museum has an exhibition of greek statues. _____

## ▶ Capitalization and Punctuation

**Draw three lines under letters that should be capital letters. Add periods where needed for abbreviations.**

In august 1963, a Baptist minister from alabama led 250,000 people in a march on washington, dc. His name was Martin luther king, jr, and his mission in life was to achieve freedom and equality for african-americans through peaceful means.

▶ **Review**

**MECHANICS**

▶ ## Punctuation in Addresses and Dates

**Rewrite these parts of a letter, adding capital letters and commas where they are needed.**

San Francisco CA 94892 _____

June 5 2001 _____

Ms. Ellen Bixby _____

American ceramics society _____

▶ ## Parentheses, Hyphens, Dashes and Ellipses

**Insert parentheses, hyphens, and dashes where they are needed in the following paragraph. Replace one punctuation mark with ellipses.**

Many warm blooded animals need extra energy to stay warm during winter. However, the food for much needed energy is not easy to find in cold weather, so the animals hibernate fall into a deep sleep all winter. A hibernating animal's body temperature falls to only a few degrees above the temperature outside. This can be as low as thirty-two degrees Fahrenheit zero degrees Celsius for a hamster. One scientist I forget which one says, "A hibernating animal, can survive the winter months without food."

▶ ## Quotation Marks, Underlining, and Apostrophes

**Insert quotation marks, underlining, and apostrophes.**

**6.** Johns favorite story, The Brave Lion, is from the book Animal Tales.

**7.** To be or not to be, William Shakespeare wrote, that is the question.

# Narrative Paragraphs

| Rule | Example |
|---|---|
| ▶ Use transition words to show readers the order in which things occur within a narrative paragraph: *then, when, next, later, early in the evening.* | |
| ▶ Include a beginning, a middle, and an end for narrative paragraphs. The beginning usually introduces what will happen in the paragraph. The middle explains the idea or describes the scene or event. The end may conclude the action or help shift the reader to the next paragraph. Dialogue may be used to help move the action forward. | ▶ Nina and Jack wondered what was behind the door and why it was always locked. Then one day, they turned the handle, and it opened. When they peered inside, they saw stacks and stacks of what looked like money. Nina looked at Jack and said, "Wow!" Next, they heard footsteps. They quickly hid and decided to explore later. |

**Try It!**

1. Number the narrative paragraph parts below. Write *1* to label the beginning, *2* for the middle, and *3* for the end.

_____ Harry and Tuny felt the water getting warmer near the large hill that had been their home base on the ocean floor. They also heard a rumbling sound. Soon they saw the other fish swimming quickly away.

_____ The ocean seemed different, and all the sea creatures were acting strangely.

_____ When they learned from the giant squid that a volcano was going to erupt, they decided to leave their overheated home and head for cooler waters.

**UNIT 6** Journeys and Quests • **Lesson 2** *Trapped by the Ice!*

▶ **Narrative Paragraphs**

**Practice**

**Underline the beginning part of each narrative paragraph below. Draw a dotted line under the middle part and draw two lines under the end. Circle any transition words that you see. (A part may consist of more than one sentence.)**

2. Tatsu knew when he went to bed that night that he would soon be in trouble. He had forgotten to mow the lawn while his father was away on a business trip, and his father would be home tomorrow. Then late at night he heard a strange, soft, shearing noise through his open window. When he looked outdoors, he saw a chimpanzee with a green cap mowing the yard with an old-fashioned push mower. He wondered where in the world this chimpanzee had come from and why he was doing his job for him.

3. Samantha opened her birthday gift. In the box was a pair of ice skates. She had never tried to skate. Days went by. She did not use her skates. Her sister finally used her skates at a nearby rink. Samantha watched and thought maybe she would skate tomorrow.

**Personal narratives are stories written about the author's own life. Write a paragraph for a personal narrative about a time you had to be polite when you didn't feel like it. Be sure to include a beginning, a middle, and an end along with transition words.**

4. _____

_____

_____

_____

_____

_____

**WRITER'S CRAFT**

# Review

## ▶ Adjectives

**Write whether each bolded adjective describes, points out, numbers, or is an article.**

1. **Many** students enjoy this class.          _____

2. She likes to sit on **that** couch.          _____

3. I found a pair of **black** gloves yesterday.          _____

4. **Twenty** boats can be seen from the harbor.          _____

5. **An** ice cube fell from the tray.          _____

6. Amelia Earhart was a **brave** woman.          _____

7. Your coat is near **the** cabinet.          _____

## ▶ Adverbs

| successfully | up | barely | often | really |
|---|---|---|---|---|

**Complete each sentence with an adverb from the box that best fits in the sentence.**

The first hot-air balloon was flown in France in 1783. It was

sent by two brothers: Jacques Etienne and Joseph Michel

Montgolfier. French statesman Leon Gambetta escaped from

Paris in a hot-air balloon during the Franco-German War of

1870. Today, however, balloons are used for recreation instead

of transportation. It would be fun to ride in a hot-air balloon!

▶ **Review**

**GRAMMAR AND USAGE**

▶ **Prepositions**

**Use these prepositions at the beginning of a prepositional phrase in a sentence.**

**8.** from _____

**9.** after _____

**10.** through _____

▶ **Conjunctions and Interjections**

**Write two sentences using coordinating conjunctions.**

**11.** _____

**12.** _____

**Write two sentences using interjections.**

**13.** _____

**14.** _____

▶ **Pronouns**

**Circle the pronouns in these sentences.**

**15.** Josie put her notebook in her backpack.

**16.** Elliot and Sarah had their lunch after they finished their chores.

**17.** Lawana, have you called your sister?

**18.** Casey and I went to his parents' house.

**19.** Winona bought a car, and she washes it every day.

**20.** When Antonio saw his brothers, he cheered for them.

**21.** Someone called for you earlier.

# Dialogue

Use dialogue in writing to involve readers, to reveal information about characters' moods and personalities, and to move the action of a story forward. Write dialogue so it sounds natural, just as people talk.

| Rule | Example |
|---|---|
| ▶ Begin the first word of a quotation with a capital letter, even if it doesn't begin the sentence. | ▶ Nicoya answered, "Everybody could do it in my old neighborhood." |
| ▶ Enclose dialogue in quotation marks and include a speaker tag showing who said it. | ▶ "Wow, where did you learn that trick?" asked Jose. |
| ▶ Place end punctuation *inside* the quotation marks. | ▶ Cassandra shouted, "Don't skate over that grate!" |
| ▶ Use slang, idioms, and occasional sentence fragments to make dialogue sound natural. | ▶ "Piece of cake," said Nicoya, smiling. |

 **Underline the sentence in each pair that has correctly punctuated dialogue. Draw a line through the sentence that has incorrect punctuation.**

1. "I think I'm going to order the fries said Keisha."
   "I think I'm going to order the fries," said Keisha.

2. "What a huge menu!" exclaimed Lindsay. "I have no idea what I want."
   "What a huge menu! exclaimed Lindsay, I have no idea what I want."

3. "You could ask the waiter what he recommends my mom said."
   "You could ask the waiter what he recommends," said my mom.

**Practice**

4. The dialogue below shows how to begin a new paragraph every time the speaker changes. Add quotation marks. Circle any slang terms, idioms, and sentence fragments that are used.

Where have you been? I've been waiting here for decades, said Tony.

I had to help my dad clean up the back alley, said Gabriel.

Well, I guess we can still play basketball, said Tony. Do you want to go to the school or to the park? There will be other kids at the park.

What's the matter? You afraid of playing me one on one? asked Gabe jokingly.

Yeah, I'm afraid I'll make so many baskets that your head will never stop spinning, laughed Tony.

**Follow the rules of writing conversation and write your own lines of dialogue.**

5. Write dialogue that has someone asking a question.

_____

6. Write dialogue in which the speaker tag is placed in the middle.

_____

7. Write two short paragraphs of dialogue showing a conversation between two speakers.

_____

_____

_____

_____

Comprehension and Language Arts Skills

WRITER'S CRAFT

# Author's Purpose

**Focus** Good readers identify the **author's purpose**, or reason, for writing a story. Identifying an author's purpose can help readers better understand the text as a whole.

An author may write:

▶ **to explain**—textbooks and how-to books are written to explain.

▶ **to inform**—reference books and other nonfiction contain informational text.

▶ **to entertain**—authors often write stories, novels, and plays to entertain.

▶ **to persuade**—advertisements, editorials, and some nonfiction books are written to persuade.

## Identify

Answer the following questions about "When Shlemiel Went to Warsaw."

**1.** What is the author's purpose for writing this tale? _____

**2.** What clues in the story help you identify this purpose? _____

_____

_____

_____

**3.** How might the story have been different if the author had

a different purpose? _____

_____

_____

_____

**Author's Purpose**

### Practice

Read each passage below. On the lines provided, write the author's purpose for each passage.

1. The attic door creaked as Anthony opened it. The light was dim, but he could see that cobwebs covered the old furniture and boxes. He walked toward a large trunk, hoping to find his old baseball bat quickly. All of a sudden— Bang!—the door to the attic slammed shut!

_____

2. Chop one head of cabbage, two carrots, and a large onion. Place the vegetables in a large pot, cover them with water, and boil them for ten minutes. Reduce the heat and add one can of stewed tomatoes, some salt, pepper, and spices. Simmer for forty-five minutes.

_____

### Apply

Write a review of "When Shlemiel Went to Warsaw." Your purpose is to persuade others to read it or not to read it.

_____

_____

_____

_____

_____

_____

_____

COMPREHENSION

**UNIT 6** Journeys and Quests • **Lesson 4** *When Shlemiel Went to Warsaw*

# Review

## ▶ Types of Sentences

**Write whether each sentence is simple, compound, or complex.**

1. Eric, who plays first base, lives on my

   street. _____

2. Ryan and his sister raised a lamb, and they are taking it to

   show at the fair. _____

3. Both Eric and Ryan live on the same street. _____

## ▶ Subject/Verb Agreement

**Cross out the incorrect verb and write the correct verb above it.**

Baseball is one of the most popular sports in the United States. Many Americans considers the game to be our national pastime. In 1869, the first professional baseball team, the Cincinnati Red Stockings, were founded. Today, each team compete to play in the World Series.

## ▶ Misused Words

**Circle the word that correctly completes each sentence.**

4. **Sit   Set**   the dishes on the counter.

5. The trip will take more time   **then   than**   you think.

6. **Can   May**   I be excused?

## Comparative and Superlative Adjectives ▶ Review

**Write the comparative and superlative forms of each adjective below.**

7. smooth _____ _____

8. heavy _____ _____

9. large _____ _____

10. good _____ _____

## ▶ Direct Objects and Indirect Objects

**Circle the direct objects and underline the indirect objects if they appear in these sentences.**

11. Please hand me the letter.

12. Patrick finished his project a week early.

13. Principal Murphy gave our class a tour of the new school.

14. My uncle sent me a post card from Europe.

## ▶ Contractions, Negatives, and Double Negatives

**Correctly rewrite these sentences that contain double negatives and add contractions.**

15. There was not nothing wrong with that calculator.

   _____

   _____

16. I do not meet them at the library no more.

   _____

   _____

GRAMMAR AND USAGE

**UNIT 6**  Journeys and Quests • **Lesson 4**  *When Shlemiel Went to Warsaw*

# Effective Beginnings and Endings

| **Rule** | **Example** |
|---|---|
| ▶ You can involve readers at the beginning of your writing by describing a **problem** that needs to be solved. | ▶ Our school is running out of classroom space, and we need more room. |
| ▶ You can involve readers at the beginning of your writing by asking a **question.** | ▶ How would you feel if your classroom was the stage in the auditorium? |
| ▶ You can end your nonfiction writing by **summarizing** your ideas in a concluding statement. | ▶ Students and their parents can help our school get more classroom space by contacting members of the school board and asking them to approve funding. |
| ▶ You can end your writing with a **final reflection** that encourages readers to think about how the information affects the world or them personally. | ▶ With adequate classroom space, students will be able to focus on their studies, and grades will improve. |

 **Write *beginning* or *ending* to show how each sentence should be used.**

1. Finally, creating music is a wonderful way to brighten

   the lives of others. _____

2. What would happen if everybody in the world drove a

   car? _____

3. Bats eat insect pests by the thousands, but scientists who study bats are noticing fewer and fewer bats every

   year. _____

**UNIT 6** Journeys and Quests • **Lesson 4** *When Shlemiel Went to Warsaw*

**Effective Beginnings and Endings**

### Practice

Begin narratives by using sensory detail and by inviting readers into the scene. Begin your expository writing by telling an interesting fact or by describing something interesting.

Write *N* (narrative) for the sentences that would make good story beginnings. Write *E* (expository) for those that would make good article beginnings.

4. _____ The strangest thing happened to my dad yesterday.

5. _____ The woods were dark and soundless, except for the distant tapping noise of elves building a cabin.

6. _____ Thirsty camels can drink up to 40 gallons of water in just a few minutes.

Imagine that you are to write an article for a school newspaper. Write the beginning and ending sentences for the topic described.

7. Write a beginning sentence that describes a problem at your school.

_____

_____

8. Write an ending that inspires a final reflection on how the same problem at school affects the reader. You may use more than one sentence.

_____

_____

_____

_____

**WRITER'S CRAFT**

# Review

## ▶ Fragments

**Write *yes* before the group of words that is a sentence.
Write *no* for the other group.**

**1.** _____ Traced back to China around A.D. 105.

**2.** _____ Millions of trees are cut down to make paper.

## ▶ Commas After Introductory Phrases

**Insert commas to separate the introductory phrase or
clause from the rest of the sentence.**

**3.** Because we were late we missed the movie previews.

**4.** In front of the mirror Juan practiced his speech for history
class.

## ▶ Punctuation and Capitalization in Friendly Letters

**Draw three lines under words that should be capitalized,
and add commas where needed in the following letter.**

> 1349 Herring road
> bangor ME 04401
> september 13 2003

dear uncle Ted and aunt Martha
    Thank you very much for the wallet you sent me for my
birthday. I miss you and hope to see you soon.

> love
> Mackenzie

**UNIT 6** Journeys and Quests • **Lesson 5** *The Search*

►**Review**

## ►Punctuation and Capitalization in Business Letters

**Circle any letters that should be capitalized and insert any commas and colons.**

50 west main street
austin TX 84281
december 1 2002

Mr. Ryan Osborn
Glossy Photos
1821 polk circle
denver CO 71446

Dear Mr. Osborn
   Thank you for the material about your program. Our committee will make our choice soon.

sincerely
*Kris Arnold*
Kris Arnold

## ►Commas with Coordinating Conjunctions

**Join the following sentences with a coordinating conjunction and a comma.**

5. One centimeter equals ten millimeters. One meter equals one hundred centimeters.

6. They will do research for the project. They will conduct the experiment.

## ►Commas with Appositives and Introductory Words

**Add commas where they are needed.**

7. Constellations groups of stars are sometimes visible in the night sky.

Comprehension and Language Arts Skills                UNIT 6 • Lesson 5   **197**

MECHANICS

**UNIT 6** Journeys and Quests • **Lesson 5** *The Search*

# Suspense

> Use suspense to make your stories more interesting, exciting, and mysterious. Readers feel suspense when they are anxious and unsure about what is going to happen next.
>
> **Rule**
> ▶ Add suspense to writing by using precise verbs, descriptive adjectives, and other exact words.
>
> ▶ Add suspense by suggesting danger.
>
> ▶ Add suspense by describing how a character feels.
>
> **Example**
> ▶ A tangle of vines crept over the crumbling ruins.
>
> ▶ A low roaring sound emerged from deep within the forest.
>
> ▶ He knew that he shouldn't be by himself in the forest at night, but it was his only chance to learn the mystery of the lost pyramid.

 **Try It!**  **Write how each sentence provides suspense. Refer to the techniques described above.**

1. Pilar had never felt so afraid in her life.

   _____

2. She shuffled her feet carefully along the crumbling ledge.

   _____

3. The crevasse below appeared to be taunting her.

   _____

4. She knew she had to control her fear.

   _____

**UNIT 6** Journeys and Quests • **Lesson 5** *The Search*

▶**Suspense**

### Practice

**Rewrite each sentence so it is more suspenseful. Add exact words, details about what characters are thinking, and other items that suggest danger.**

**5.** Ling Chin bent down so the others wouldn't see her.

_____

**6.** Nick wondered whether he should walk back.

_____

**7.** She saw something out of the corner of her eye.

_____

**8.** Liam found old coins at the bottom of a chest.

_____

**9.** The lake appeared rougher than usual.

_____

**Create your own suspense by writing original sentences.**

**10.** Write about an actual or imaginary time that you hid from someone.

_____

_____

_____

_____

_____

_____

**WRITER'S CRAFT**

# Review

## Sentences and Punctuation

**Draw three lines under any letters that should be capitalized and add correct end punctuation. Change fragments by adding words or making them part of another sentence.**

In 1769, on the 5,000 acres he inherited from his father, Thomas Jefferson started work on his house, Monticello! Spending 40 years designing, building, re-creating, and adding to his fabulous home. He was a stickler for details. in 1794, he started redesigning the house? Wanted the two-story house to appear as a single story! Jefferson made sure everything was just how he wanted it, especially the furniture. Of some of the furniture. he devised some of the home's gadgets: a dumbwaiter, a clock that marked the days of the week, and a revolving service door with shelves!

## Subjects and Predicates

**Underline the complete subject and circle the complete predicate.**

1. The writer Charles Dickens was born on February 7, 1812.

2. The English novelist is considered to be one of the greatest of his time.

3. Many people still read his stories today.

4. One of my friends wrote a report about Charles Dickens.

5. *A Christmas Carol* is my favorite story by Dickens.

▶**Review**

## ▶ Direct and Indirect Objects

**Circle the direct objects and underline any indirect objects in the following sentences.**

6. Lakes provide water for many uses.

7. Rainwater filled a volcanic crater in Oregon to form Crater Lake.

8. My uncle gave me the Virginia state quarter for my collection.

9. Please give us a call when you get home.

## ▶ Subject/Verb Agreement

**Rewrite these sentences, correcting subject/verb agreement and double negatives.**

10. His example doesn't make no sense to me.

   _____

   _____

11. Forest fires destroys millions of trees each year.

   _____

   _____

12. The class want to take another field trip to the museum.

   _____

   _____

GRAMMAR, USAGE, AND MECHANICS

**UNIT 6**  Journeys and Quests • **Lesson 6** *Alberic the Wise*

# Point of View

### Rule

▶ Use the first-person point of view when you want one of the characters in the story to tell the story. The first-person narrator uses the pronouns *I, me, my, we, us,* and *our* to describe his or her involvement in the story.

▶ Use the first-person point of view when you want readers to identify with or feel close to the narrating character.

▶ Use the third-person point of view when the narrator is not involved in the story. Use the pronouns *he, she, they, them, him,* and *her* to describe what characters say and do.

▶ The third-person point of view allows the narrator to describe the thoughts and feelings of one character, several characters, or none of the characters.

 **Write *first person* or *third person* to label the point of view used.**

1. _____ We never thought we would reach the other side. Carly had a sprained ankle, and I had blisters covering every inch of my feet.

2. _____ Max and Edie were best friends even though one was a cat and one was a dog. The two acted as if they didn't know they belonged to totally different species.

3. _____ Kailey wondered if they were on the right street, and Jared worried that they weren't even in the right neighborhood.

4. _____ It wasn't that I didn't like the idea of exploring the ravine; I just didn't want to do it so soon after the accident.

**UNIT 6** Journeys and Quests • **Lesson 6** *Alberic the Wise*

▶ **Point of View**

**Practice**

**Which point of view would you use? Write *first person* or *third person*.**

5. You want readers to identify closely with the main

   character. _____

6. You want to be able to describe the thoughts and feelings

   of all of the characters in the story. _____

7. You want to use the pronoun *I* for telling the story.

   _____

8. You want to describe what is going on inside the heads of

   just two of the characters in a story. _____

**Write a short paragraph that could be part of a larger story. Use the first-person point of view to describe what a main character thinks, says, and does.**

9. _____

   _____

   _____

   _____

**Write a paragraph that could be part of a longer story, using the third-person point of view to describe what characters think, say, and do.**

10. _____

   _____

   _____

   _____

WRITER'S CRAFT